Advance P

Christian Medical and Dental Associations (CMDA) works on 242 medical/dental school campuses with over ten thousand students. I wish I could give each one of them this book! It contains the secrets of having contentment, academic success, a balanced life, and most importantly, a focus on Christ during your challenging days of training. Its insights and advice are invaluable. If you are a future or present med student, it should be at the top of your reading list—or you can just learn what it contains the hard way! I'm an overachiever and highly competitive like you—I wish I'd had this book when I was in medical school. In an atmosphere of pressure to master seemingly unlimited knowledge, that often becomes the recipe for depression, cynicism, spiritual stagnation, a radically unbalanced life, and, ultimately, burnout. *Beyond Studying* contains the secrets for avoiding those traps. If you apply them, you will not just survive but flourish!

—David Stevens MD, MA, chief executive officer, Christian Medical & Dental Associations

In *Beyond Studying*, Eric Huang and Richard Chung provide a thoughtful, accessible, and practical companion to medical students who want to maintain and deepen their faith. A particular strength is the way in which they organize the book around the major phases and milestones of medical school, each with its decisional and emotional demands. Another is the organization of each chapter into a discussion of the spiritual dimension of these issues, a related prayer, and suggested questions for reflection. Still a third is the use by the authors of their own humbling and instructive experiences to encourage the development of life-long habits of balanced and fulfilling service. *Beyond Studying* is a fresh and valuable resource for both individuals and groups committed to following Jesus into the world of medicine.

—John R. Peteet, MD, associate professor of psychiatry, Harvard Medical School, Dana-Farber Cancer Institute

Dr. Huang has blessed us with a book that goes "beyond studying"— and even beyond the medical profession. His exploration of spirituality (in his case, Christian) in medical school could well apply to any graduate student as they wrestle to discern their calling. And while his inquiry is structured by the four years of medical school, it truly extends to the residency and practice that follows. In writing that "prioritizing God above medicine, or anything for that matter, is truly unconventional living," he has written a truly unconventional book. He reflects that "after everything was said and done, I was in medical school to demonstrate God's love and compassion and minister effectively to those around me, whether they were patients, fellow students, or even the dean of the faculty." One can't help but hope that someday Dr. Huang himself might become the dean of a medical school, shaping a culture where expressing spirituality is a valued and vibrant norm.

—John R. Knight, MD, associate professor of pediatrics, Harvard Medical School; senior associate in medicine, associate in psychiatry, Children's Hospital Boston

Beyond Studying is highly practical, not just for medical students but for anyone thinking about a career in health care. Figuring out God's will for you is one thing. Actually carrying it out when the training is done is another challenge altogether. This book is a wonderful resource for all believers who desire to nurture their relationship with the Lord amidst the rigors of medical training.

—Jack Tsai, MD, family physician, author of *Worth the Cost? Becoming a Doctor Without Forfeiting Your Soul*

Beyond Studying

A Guide to Faith, Life, and Learning for
Students in Health-Care Professions

Praying Luke 10:27
for you.

ERIC HUANG, MD

RICHARD CHUNG, MD

WESTBOW®
PRESS
A DIVISION OF THOMAS NELSON
& ZONDERVAN

Scriptures taken from the Holy Bible, New International Version®, NIV®. Copyright © 1973, 1978, 1984, 2011 by Biblica, Inc.™ Used by permission of Zondervan. All rights reserved worldwide. www.zondervan.com The "NIV" and "New International Version" are trademarks registered in the United States Patent and Trademark Office by Biblica, Inc.™ All rights reserved.

Scripture quotations taken from the Holy Bible, New Living Translation, copyright 1996, 2004. Used by permission of Tyndale House Publishers, Inc., Wheaton, Illinois 60189. All rights reserved.

Scripture quotations are from The Holy Bible, English Standard Version® (ESV®), copyright © 2001 by Crossway, a publishing ministry of Good News Publishers. Used by permission. All rights reserved.

All Scripture quotations in this publications are from **The Message**. Copyright (c) by Eugene H. Peterson 1993, 1994, 1995, 1996, 2000, 2001, 2002. Used by permission of NavPress Publishing Group.

WestBow Press books may be ordered through booksellers or by contacting:

WestBow Press
A Division of Thomas Nelson & Zondervan
1663 Liberty Drive
Bloomington, IN 47403
www.westbowpress.com
1 (866) 928-1240

Because of the dynamic nature of the Internet, any web addresses or links contained in this book may have changed since publication and may no longer be valid. The views expressed in this work are solely those of the author and do not necessarily reflect the views of the publisher, and the publisher hereby disclaims any responsibility for them.

Any people depicted in stock imagery provided by Thinkstock are models, and such images are being used for illustrative purposes only. Certain stock imagery © Thinkstock.

ISBN: 978-1-4908-2999-9 (sc)
ISBN: 978-1-4908-3000-1 (hc)
ISBN: 978-1-4908-2998-2 (e)

Library of Congress Control Number: 2014904818

Printed in the United States of America.

WestBow Press rev. date: 03/21/2014

Contents

Preface

Despite having a father and two older brothers who practiced medicine, my world was turned upside down and inside out when I entered medical school. Studying, I was surprised to find, no longer meant just going to classes, doing the assigned homework, and carrying on with the rest of my life. The amount of time I needed to study (which was never quite enough), the seemingly limitless energy required to make it through rotations, and the sheer volume of data I needed to absorb slowly began sucking away at who I was and who I thought I wanted to become.

But I also understood the sacrifices I had to make. After all, this would become my life's work! So, despite some hesitation, I threw myself into it. While dealing with the pressing matters of each day, I tried to give God his due. But as the years went by, I could feel that I was pushing him more and more into the periphery, while I stood at center stage.

After my third year of medical school, I stepped away from the rigors of rotations to do research in Boston, Massachusetts. During that time, I began wondering, *Is there a better way? Why is it so hard to be a Christian in medical school? And why do I so easily give in to my self-centered ambition and desires?* Around this time, I also found out that several of my friends who had gone through or were in medical school had abandoned their faith and were living lifestyles that demonstrated their rejection of God. Interestingly enough, they all had been leaders of their Christian fellowships in college, and I remembered looking up to them for what seemed to be unshakable faith. Just what was it about medical school that turned these faithful followers of Christ into bitter, often angry rebels? As I look back, I see that I too was headed down that same path. It was only by God's grace and mercy, and the fellowship of godly friends, that he kept me.

During my year in Boston, I met Richard, a fellow medical student, who also was taking time off to do research. With his encouragement, his deep and passionate faith, and some thought and prayer together, the idea of writing a book that addressed the issues we faced as Christian medical students was born. You may be familiar with the many books that have been written about how to get into medical school, but very few of them really address the student's life—especially a Christian's life—while actually in medical school.

Although noble in purpose, the process of learning medicine can be very taxing on both the soul and body. As I learned from personal experience, a tired soul begins, over time, to live for self and not for God. Ungodly habits and perspectives can sink deep into a person's heart, and once medical school is completed, he emerges as a weak and defeated Christian who—albeit with medical degree in hand—no longer considers God his hunger, hope, or ultimate desire. Instead, the bottom line is his need to keep up with the Joneses, and building a personal kingdom becomes the impetus for getting out of bed every morning.

This crucible of faith is particularly hot in the midst of our training, whether we are in medical school or residency. The culture of medicine is one that we must navigate with open eyes, a strong mind, and a heart that is desperately reliant upon God for daily strength. The goal of this book is to provide a solid foundation of hope for you. Both Richard and I hope that the biblical principles, meditations, and practical suggestions offered here will, by God's grace, help you to see beyond the urgency of the moment and cultivate a godward life that gives God the glory he deserves. We pray that, as you trust in him, you would persevere mightily for the sake of his kingdom and for your soul.

—Eric Huang, MD

Acknowledgments

There are many who have contributed to this endeavor, and the many lives that have touched mine have been both spiritually and professionally encouraging.

Richard, this book would never have been written had it not been for your brotherly encouragement and contribution.

Thank you, Daniel Huang, Bob Mason, and Jack Tsai for your incredibly helpful wisdom and guidance, especially as the book was being finalized.

Heidi Walker (Strong Tower Publishing), your editing services and kind words of encouragement have been a source of joyful motivation for me.

Josh Sung, your fresh eyes and insights have made this book invaluable for students wanting to go into the medical profession.

And Lord, thank you for giving those of us working in the health-care profession the greatest reason for doing the work we do.

CHAPTER 1

Your Spiritual Walk

My introduction to anatomy class began, as it did for every first-year medical student, by receiving a large, rectangular, wooden briefcase. As the professor called our names, he handed us these heavy but unimpressive-looking containers held shut by two fading, slightly rusted metal clasps. Grasping the plastic handle, I felt as if I were taking a trip back to the 1930s.

"Ladies and gentlemen," my professor began, peering over his wire-rimmed glasses. He looked left to right across the classroom, as if he wanted to catch all our reactions at the same time. "You will have these cases for the entire semester. You may take them home. Just don't open them in the middle of the street." Seeing the somewhat confused faces in front of him, he added mischievously, "Open them up."

As we flipped the clasps open, the room was filled with chuckles and soft gasps. There before us lay real human bones: a skull; an entire spinal column of vertebrae held together by fishing wire; and the bones of a hand, leg, and torso. One student wondered aloud what would happen if, on our way home, campus police stopped us and asked what was in the box. "Nothing, officer ... just, er, some human remains?"

When I first started medical school, I was enthralled by what was taught. Exploring the body and its functions was a fascinating, new, and exciting experience. Learning the Latin names given to each nook and cranny of a bone, or looking at my own hand and being able to identify each part anatomically, was intellectually stimulating. But it didn't take long to feel overwhelmed by the sheer volume of material I was expected to learn. Someone estimated that in the first year alone, medical students learn almost thirteen thousand new vocabulary words! It was like trying to drink water from a fire hydrant. The amount of time I needed to study, coupled with the daily grind of classes, wore away at my quiet time with God, my desire to meet with other believers, and my hunger to be used by God to further his kingdom. The wear and tear left me with a ragged desire simply to survive.

I knew, though, that maintaining my spiritual walk could not simply be achieved by knowing principles about the Christian life or doing things Christians usually do. In other words, going to Christian meetings, volunteering at the free clinic, or participating in Sunday services could all be done with an empty heart and a cold soul—that is, in vain. While wonderful and important in themselves, these acts of service were not enough to maintain a vibrant, growing, and humble faith. The issue was one of the heart. And I knew things had to change.

In college, I had led Bible studies, discipled students, played bass in the worship band, and been on the leadership team for my fellowship. But in medical school, I soon realized that I had nowhere near as much time to spend on my spiritual growth as I'd once had. College had afforded me the time to grow in my faith. But now the task was daunting, and my efforts were feeble and easily swept aside by the busyness of my new life. I wasn't prepared for the lack of time and the dearth of believers in my classes. As it turned out, the pressures of medical school became a litmus test for revealing exactly what I was made of, and things did not look good!

Whenever my heart of love and worship for the Lord grew cold, service became a thankless offering and even an underhanded way to build my *own* kingdom rather than God's. The struggles I experienced revealed my selfish desires and ambitions. Paul Tripp, a Christian author and counselor, said it well: "If the heart doesn't change, the person's words and behavior may change temporarily because of an external pressure or incentive. But when the pressure or incentive is removed, the changes will disappear."[1] This was particularly true for me. Without the consistent fellowship and daily disciplines that a college organization or a set of faithful friends provided, the priorities of my heart began to reveal themselves more fully.

Who He Is

When I entered medical school, I had two things going against me. School left me little time and energy to spend on nourishing my spiritual life, and my heart's natural tendency was to seek things other than God. In the midst of all this, how could I possibly maintain a vital, flourishing relationship with Christ?

Have you ever heard an inspiring sermon or uplifting talk that stirred you to worship God more passionately? If so, you know it is more than a fleeting feeling. You were brought to a genuine conviction, because you understood a particular aspect of God's character and his relationship with you more fully. That conviction may have left you humbled, inspired, or reenergized, as you enjoyed anew the magnificent greatness of God. Moments like these teach us that what drives us to worship wholeheartedly is knowing more deeply who God is.

In Tripp's book, *Instruments in the Redeemer's Hands*, he describes three attributes of God that believers—especially those who feel dry, stagnant, or spiritually parched (like students struggling through medical school)—can meditate on to allow their souls to draw from a deeply satisfying and life-giving wellspring. These attributes are God's sovereignty, grace, and glory.

God's Sovereignty

I began many days praying, "May my life now be a sacrifice to you." But by evening, my plea often became, "Oh Lord, just sacrifice me now!"

If you don't want your faith to falter, you must first realize that faith cannot begin with you. It cannot even begin with your longing or your self-generated desire to worship God. Our own initiative to glorify and honor him is too fickle and inconsistent (Rom. 3:10–12). Thankfully and amazingly, whether in our moments of disobedient opposition or joyful love for him, it is ultimately God's sovereign power that accomplishes his purposes for our lives. Daniel 4:34–35 describes it this way: "His dominion is an eternal dominion ... He does as he pleases ... No one can hold back his hand or say to him: 'What have you done?'"

According to Tripp, God is saying, "Take heart, I am in complete control. I am the definition of holiness and love. All of my ways are right and true; all of my decisions are the best; and I will not rest until my plan has been completed." Tripp continues: "A Christian's inner peace is never based on his ability to take the teachings of Scripture and figure it all out. Our peace always rests on the presence, power, and character of the Lord."[2]

Trusting in God's sovereignty will give you the strength to live for him in the midst of medical school and beyond. When you congratulate a fellow medical student on her successful exam, despite your own struggles in that class; when you fight the temptation to put your classmates at a disadvantage by hoarding or not sharing your resources (there are sad stories of students who have refused to share class notes or who have checked out books at the library only to hold on to them so others cannot access them); when you go to bed after a long day of studying, despite feeling that you still have much more to do and yet echo in faith the words of David: "I will lie down and sleep in peace, for you alone, O Lord, make me dwell in safety" (Ps. 4:8)—when you do these things, then you are resting in the sovereignty of God.

If you are anything like me—fretting over the stress of everyday life, completing my studies, and maintaining spiritual well-being—then think and dwell upon how resting in the absolute, unshakable sovereignty of God can provide a confident and peaceful assurance in which you can hope. Listen: God's loving authority and power over you and your future is even more certain than the sun rising tomorrow.

God's Grace

God's grace, or his unmerited favor, has permeated history from the beginning of time. After Adam and Eve disobeyed God's command not to eat from the tree of knowledge, they brought judgment and the curse of death upon themselves and their posterity. However, in Genesis 3:15, we read that God immediately made it known that he would provide a way to redeem them. "Because of his great love for us, God, who is rich in mercy, made us alive with Christ even when we were dead in transgressions—it is by grace you have been saved" (Eph. 2:4–5).

Even though we all carry the sinful nature given to us by Adam, Jesus brings those who acknowledge him as Savior from death into everlasting life. These truths from his Word are a reminder that God's loving grace is not dependent upon our own worthiness, how well we perform academically, or how intellectually astute we appear before others. I admit that many times I felt like a failure when I didn't do well on an exam or was intimidated by my classmates' successes. At those times, I found it helpful to remember this: while I am still a sinner with nothing to offer him, Christ still willingly died for me (Rom. 5:8). How could I feel down about myself when this incredibly selfless, undeserved love had been lavished upon me?

Grace not only reveals God's faithful heart, but it also empowers us to live by it, even in our weakest moments. "For the grace of God … teaches us to say 'No' to ungodliness and worldly passions, and to live self-controlled, upright and godly lives in this present age, while we wait for the blessed hope—the glorious appearing of our great God and Savior, Jesus Christ, who gave himself for us to redeem us from all wickedness and to purify for himself a people that are his very own, eager to do what is good (Titus 2:11–14).

God's grace allows us to respond to our circumstances in God-honoring ways. It enables us to see beyond our horizontally limited human perspectives and allow the vertical dimension of God's grace to immensely expand our field of vision and hope for the future.

When we are floundering in class, God's grace gives us hope, because we know that through such struggles God is creating in us a holy perseverance and character to display his glory. Correspondingly, an honors grade does not cause us to become prideful, because we remember that any blessing we receive comes from the Father, who has already given us his Son and who graciously gives us all things (Rom. 8:32).

God's grace allows us to offer love and genuine concern to those whose competitive natures have isolated them from others—or to give that classmate who seems to have a hidden agenda the benefit of the doubt. (Don't forget that we can fall into these temptations too!) God's grace enables us to extend seemingly irrational love and kindness to others (irrational in the sense of: "Why should I care for you, if you only care about yourself?"), because "God chose the foolish things of the world to shame the wise; God chose the weak things of the world to shame the strong" (1 Cor. 1:27).

God wants you to show the incomparable riches of his grace, not necessarily by being a top scorer or high ranking achiever in your class, but in how you display his grace through the interactions and everyday work he puts before you. It is both empowering and essential to remember God's grace when you study with classmates, receive test scores, eat in the cafeteria, or pore over your textbooks. Fix his unreserved grace within your heart, and you will find yourself echoing the truths of an old gospel spiritual by Mahalia Jackson: "Lord, don't move the mountain. Just give me the strength to climb." Living in God's comforting and liberating grace gives you the power to rejoice deeply with God and others, whatever the circumstances.

God's Glory

When I first started medical school, I asked God boldly, "What would you have me do? Your servant is listening." But as the long, grueling months of relentless study wore on, there were many times when I did not feel like praying, fellowshipping, or meditating on God's Word. My spiritual vision was slowly but surely dimming. My prayers became more like, "Lord, could you maybe just let me do my thing for now? Surely you understand. Your servant is getting tired."

I think many believers have the idea that falling away from one's faith involves a spectacular crash-and-burn, so they believe themselves to be immune. In reality, such falls are usually more insidious.

Compromise often begins with baby steps. For me, it began with thinking, "If I try to be a good doctor and work hard, that is all that really matters, right?" Those are worthy goals, no doubt, but how was that mind-set any different from those of my nonbelieving classmates? Veiled in that seemingly honorable statement was this belief: "God is important, but right now I'm too busy doing my own thing. Maybe I'll fit God in somehow—but later."

Your understanding of what it means to be a doctor is molded by your experiences, but every experience is meant to give glory to the Lord. Romans 11:36 makes it clear: "For from him and through him and to him are all things. To him be the glory forever!" Believe it or not, working hard and being kind or competent only for our own sakes is an exercise in self-glorification. C. S. Lewis pointed out this challenging (and shocking) truth in *Mere Christianity*:

> If you are a nice person—if virtue comes easily to you—beware! Much is expected from those [to] whom much is given. If you mistake for your own merits what are really God's gifts to you through nature, and if you are contented with simply being nice, you are still a rebel: and all those gifts will only make your fall more terrible, your corruption more complicated, your bad example more disastrous. The Devil was an archangel once; his natural gifts were far above yours as yours are above those of a chimpanzee.[3]

Lewis was saying that, as much as you might want to convince yourself that being a nice, helpful person or a diligent, hard worker is all that matters, such work becomes self-glorifying, which, simply put, is rebellious idolatry. Instead, let your accomplishments and experiences be done with the purpose of reflecting any glory you might receive back to God, acknowledging that all the work you do is for his glory and for his sake and in his strength. Only in humble reliance upon Christ can you love and care for others in a w pleases and worships him. In the way you take care of patients, interact with colleagues, and pursue wholeness in your personal life, let these bring out the Redeemer's ways, truths, and practices, which usher in his kingdom on earth. Whatever accolades, awards, or letters you get after your name, remember that a truly fulfilling life can only be experienced by living for his glory, not your own.

Suggested Prayer

"Lord, thank you for this opportunity to be a medical student. I pray that I would not rest in how strong my spiritual life has been in the past. I pray that instead I would be a faithful follower of Jesus Christ in my years of training here. I know that medical school can challenge and change me. May it change me to be more like you. Let my life and my studies be an outpouring of my worship to you. Help me to be guided by the comfort of your sovereignty, knowing that you have all things under your loving control, both good and bad.

"Let me be strengthened by your grace. You gave me your only Son that I might have the strength and power to live for you, even in the hard times. Let me live for your glory. As much as medical school may tempt me to live for my own gain, remind me that anything done in selfish interest is prideful, rebellious to your loving and gracious character, and ultimately unfulfilling. Instead, fill me with your Holy Spirit. May he give me true joy and satisfaction as I trust you today."

Questions to Ponder

1. What aspects of medical school (such as people, time, material to be learned) do you find challenging to your spiritual growth?

2. How does resting in God's sovereignty inform your approach to your studies and relationships with your classmates?

3. What is it about God's grace that can give you confidence and humility when you feel as if you don't measure up or that you are superior to your classmates?

4. How does God's grace encourage you to genuinely love your classmates? How can you give grace to them today?

5. How does God's glory, as described by C. S. Lewis, put to death the thought: "If I try to be a good doctor and work hard at my calling, that is all that really matters"? What can you do to give God glory today?

Chapter 1 Endnotes

1. Paul Tripp, *Instruments in the Hands of the Redeemer* (Phillipsburg, N.J.: Presbyterian & Reformed Publishing Co., 2002), 62.

2. Ibid., 30.

3. C. S. Lewis, *The Complete C. S. Lewis Signature Classics* (New York: HarperOne), 169.

CHAPTER 2

Spiritual Stepping Stones

I recently spent a weekend at a Christian retreat nestled in the woods near Yosemite National Park in California. It was early summer, late at night, and as a group of us looked up toward the sky, the crickets sang cheerfully to us. As the stars twinkled brightly and the full moon fell low on the horizon, I was able to make out two bright planets—a yellow one and a red one. Of course, they looked tiny to the unaided eye, but with the aid of a telescope someone had brought along, Saturn's beige-colored rings and Mars' deep-red surface suddenly came into crisp view. What initially seemed so small and insignificant had been corrected, and we could begin to see how big they truly were.

Magnify Him!

John Piper gives an excellent analogy of what it means to magnify God.[1] It is not like looking through a microscope and examining a miniscule drop of blood for schistocytes. (You'll have plenty of tir in pathology class for that.) Such a process makes something ' small appear larger than it actually is.

Magnifying God is like looking through a telescope int' night sky, making that which looks small begin to app' it actually is. To the naked eye, for example, Jupiter is just a blip in the sky. A telescope gives us an understanding of its proper size—in this case, a volume more than fourteen hundred times that of Earth. In the same way, when we magnify God, we show others (and ourselves) who may think little of him how big he really is.

Piper described it well: "The whole duty of the Christian can be summed up in this: feel, think, and act in a way that will make God look as great as he really is. Be a telescope for the world of the infinite starry wealth of the glory of God."[2] Ask God to give you a vision of his wisdom, power, and goodness so that you can magnify him through your life.

Meditate on God's Word

A resident I knew once said, "In your undergraduate years, you make sure you don't omit Jesus from your life, but in medical school, make sure you commit to Jesus with your life." What he meant was that, in terms of time, it is easier to spend time with God in college than in medical school, where as each year presses on, the work piles up, and there seems to be less and less time for God. I certainly found this to be true for me. It was easy to skim through a couple of verses or to read a short devotional in the morning—and then to forget everything I'd read, the moment I closed the door to my apartment on the way to class.

Reading the Bible every day is a great start for your spiritual walk, but it is only when we really absorb his Word into our hearts that it can cause lasting change in our lives. There is no magic involved. When God's Word is taken deep into our hearts, the Spirit brings the light of truth to our experiences and changes us. Instead of being consumed by our day-to-day worries, we get a perspective from

God's point of view, and insight into how we can be a part of what God is actively doing in the world.

One thing I found that helped me meditate on his Word during the day was to take an index card and write down a verse that had impressed me that morning. Then I stuck the card into my pocket and went back to it several times throughout the day. I also took advantage of apps on my phone to keep God's Word near (more on this in chapter 15). I read these verses between patients when rounding, before noon conference started, or at the end of the day as I was getting into the car to go home. Having these verses continually percolating in my brain throughout the day did wonders to keep my heart on track. St. Ignatius of Loyola wrote:

> The devil cannot take from the soul the light of faith: he, however, removes the light of consideration; so that the soul may not reflect on what it believes. And as it is of no avail to open the eyes in the dark, so says St. Augustine, "it is of no advantage to be near the light if the eyes are closed." The eternal maxims, considered in the light of faith, are most clear; yet if we do not open the eyes of the mind by meditating on them, we live as if we were perfectly blind; and so precipitate ourselves into every vice.[3]

Open your eyes to God's heart-changing Word by meditating on his character—his sovereignty, grace, and glory. You will find that doing so will provide deep spiritual nourishment that will strengthen you.

Growing without Qualifications

Have you ever found yourself saying things like, "As long as my grades are good, I'll go to church," or "As long as I don't get behind in my work, I'll keep doing my devotionals," or "As long as my attending likes me, I'll keep a cheerful heart for God"? In other words, have you been tempted to set conditions for your spiritual growth? I know I have. I faced this often, and it took me a while to understand that I could not let my status in life determine my obedience to God.

When we begin to see the incredible greatness and glory of God, it becomes a deeply joyful, sensible, and God-glorifying thing to fit medicine into the paradigm of faith, rather than the other way around. Saying something like, "As long as I'm doing well in school, then I'll honor God" makes no sense and reveals our backward thinking. Fight this temptation by purposing in your heart to obey him, regardless of your circumstances, and to magnify him to the fullest by meditating on his greatness and goodness.

Suggested Prayer

"Father, you are the Creator of all things, from the tiniest particle to the farthest reaches of the universe. I pray that I would not see you as just *part* of my life but as the *reason* for my life. You created it all! Please help me to magnify you in every aspect of my life, to reveal how truly awesome, glorious, and holy you are. I pray for understanding and eyes to see that it makes no sense to let the events of my day determine whether or not I obey you. In my weakness, I know I cannot do it on my own, so I ask your Spirit to give me strength to live wholly for you. I want to purposefully meditate on your Word throughout the day. Let it be held close to my heart so that I do not forget it easily. Let your Word be my hope, strength, and help always."

Questions to Ponder

1. It is easy to compromise in your heart: "As long as I don't get behind on my work, then I'll keep my devotional time with God." What other excuses or rationalizations do you make when you let your status in life dictate your obedience to God? How can you prevent yourself from slipping into this mentality?

2. What ways can you, like a telescope, show how great God really is? Think about his wisdom, power, and goodness. Give him thanks and praise as you think about each of these characteristics and how each relates to the world around you and to your own life specifically.

3. What steps can you take to purposefully meditate on God's Word this week? Can you take an extra five minutes and find a place of solace sometime during the day to do this?

Chapter 2 Endnotes

1. John Piper gives a wonderful sermon regarding what it means to magnify God, using the analogy of microscope and telescope. You can listen to the sermon online on John Piper's website, *Desiring God*, at http://www.desiringgod.org/resource-library/sermons/i-will-magnify-god-with-thanksgiving.

2. Ibid.

3. St. Ignatius of Loyola, "The Spiritual Exercises of St. Ignatius, with Meditations and Prayers," *New Cyclopaedia of Prose Illustrations: Adapted to Christian Teaching: Embracing Allegories, Analogies, Anecdotes, Aphorisms, Emblems, Fables, Legends, Metaphors, Parables, Quotations, Similes, Biblical Types and Figures, Etc.* (Google Books), 707.

CHAPTER 3

Studying (for) God in Medical School

Do get on with your studies. Remember you are now forming
the character of your future ministry. If you acquire slovenly or
sleepy habits of study now, you will never get the better of it. Do
everything in earnest—if it is worth doing, then do it with all your
might. Above all, keep much in the presence of God. Never see
the face of man till you have seen His face who is our life, our all.
—Letter to a student from Scottish minister
Robert Murray M'Cheyne, 1840

I remember unzipping the large, white, elongated plastic bag and
catching a glimpse of what I would be working on for months to
come. It was my first day of anatomy lab. I remember the smell of
fixative permeating the room (to the point that I wondered if it
would embalm my brain too). The initial shock from poring over,
poking at, and dissecting a human cadaver stayed with me for several
days. It took even longer to get the smell out of my nose!

At first, we were all tentative with our scalpels, grimacing as we
incised and peeled away layers of cold, gray skin and the liquid-soft,
butter-colored fat. I remember thinking, as I dissected the pectoralis
muscle, "This looks strangely and uncomfortably like the slices of

roast beef I just bought at Stop & Shop" (which, by the way, I very soon stopped eating!).

When it came time to enter the heart and lungs, many of my classmates looked away, while the more daring wielded bone saws and cut through the rib cage to reveal the vital organs. It was in those moments that you could, with some degree of certainty, point out the budding orthopedic surgeons, as their eyes lit up while they held the buzzing, humming power tools in their hands. As the days grew to weeks, however, everyone began easing into the rigors of pulling apart fascia, exposing organs, and appreciating more fully the complexity of the human body.

There are myriad books, programs, and guides that can help you with techniques for studying, but as a Christian medical student, even more important than studying itself is studying in a way that honors God. If every aspect of our lives—even down to the most basic tasks, like eating and drinking—can be done in a way that glorifies him (1 Cor. 10:31), then surely studying (and even dissecting cadavers) can reflect his greatness and glory too.

For the Christian, studying is not a secular activity, although it may often feel that way. You are not called to "hurry up and finish studying so you can then do the really godly things." I used to think this way. I thought that the things I did needed to be explicitly "Christian" in order for them to be truly pleasing to God. Instead, I came to understand that the line between secular and religious pursuits was unhealthy to draw. Indeed, such lines had no place in my life at all.

The Irish poet Evangeline Paterson described it well: "I was brought up in a Christian environment where, because God had to be given pre-eminence, nothing else was allowed to be important. I have broken through to the position that because God exists, everything has significance."[1]

Obeying the command to love the Lord with our minds (Matt. 22:37; Mark 12:30; Luke 10:27) gives glory to God and eternal significance to our studying—yes, eternal significance! John Calvin addressed the incorrect understanding that to be a Christian means having permission not to use our God-given intellectual capabilities for his glory or to be unlearned in life: "By 'being fools' we do not mean being stupid; nor do we direct those who are learned in the liberal sciences to jettison their knowledge, and those who are gifted with quickness of mind to become dull, as if a man cannot be a Christian unless he is more like a beast than a man. The profession of Christianity requires us to be immature, not in our thinking, but in malice."[2]

We study, then, not only to retain information but to actually worship God, because we are doing what he has created and called us to do. This should be our motivation for being diligent in our studies. We can study hard and well—for his glory!

A Different Attitude

You may find yourself, along with other medical students, complaining about how much needs to be studied and learned (and there is more than enough, no doubt), but as a Christian, it is important to understand that the attitude with which you study gives glory to God even more than the results. I often grumbled about the work thrown upon me and the unfair expectation to remember it all. I found myself longing for days of old when I had been able to sleep all day and stay up all night.

It was easy to fall into this mentality because of the intense studying required, but over time, I began to consider seriously the challenging call God had given me to serve him in this unique role. Yes, there are many costs to becoming a doctor, but before we begin to complain about how much we are being spent, we should remember Amy Carmichael's words: "Satan is so much more in earnest than we are—he buys up the opportunity while we are wondering how much it will cost."[3] Don't let the evil one take advantage of your time and energy. Offer up your studies as daily opportunities to glorify God.

The right attitude in medicine does not mean pulling yourself up by your cerebral bootstraps and working yourself into the ground. It involves obediently trusting the one who gave you that calling in the first place and who promises to strengthen you in everything you do (Phil 4:13). This truth has serious spiritual ramifications. Here are some heart attitudes you can ask the Lord to help maintain in you as you study.

Come humbly.

Remind yourself that you belong to him. Come before the Lord without self-imposed limitations, without a personal agenda, and lay prostrate in your heart before him, asking: "What do you have in mind for me now as I begin studying?" Ask God to take precedence. Entrust to him your time and ask that he guide and direct your mind. Responsibly undertake what God has given you to do with the gifts he has bestowed upon you. Refuse to cut short the stewardship God expects of you. Remember, it is worship when you study.

At the same time, beware of false humility. If you are struggling in your studies, do not accuse yourself by saying things like, "I'm so stupid. I can't remember all this," or "Everyone gets this but me. I'm such an idiot!" This is not true humility. Such feelings only lead to feelings of worthlessness, frustration, and despair that undermine

19

your studies and worship of God. The battle for the mind begins with refusing to believe subtle lies that are ultimately evil in nature. Instead, ask the Lord to help you internalize his acceptance of you. Not believing that you are loved and completely accepted by him denies the costly sacrifice required of God to bring you into his amazing grace. You have been forgiven and accepted. Claim it! Jesus Christ is your greatest advocate.

Be wary of being consumed by your daily workload.

It is easy to become myopic about the daily problems that present themselves before you and to ignore the spiritual warfare around you. The battle against your workload is not your primary struggle. It is the struggle to let the Holy Spirit fight the battle in your stead.

Don't suffer in your studies in the name of God and yet walk away from him at the same time. It is he who promises to strengthen you with all power so that you might have great endurance and patience to live a life worthy of him (Col. 1:10–11). Ask him to help you maintain sight of the big picture. The smaller our vision of God, the greater the likelihood that our daily problems will consume us.

God's purpose is to advance his kingdom in the world by changing the hearts and minds of people, starting with those of his children. Remember the ultimate purpose of your life and live it accordingly. You don't want to hit a roadblock someday and ask yourself, "Why in the world am I doing this?" Don't lose the forest for the trees.

Engage the world.

Success in medical school is a function of being engaged in it. I often found myself struggling with a survivalist mentality that tempted me to hide my faith or shed it to some degree as I got caught up in the worries of staying on top of my workload and wanting to be accepted by my classmates. Before I could understand *who* I was (a medical student involved in professional training), I needed to understand *whose* I was—God's beloved. God had placed me in medical school for the purpose of glorifying him. My primary motivation was to live for him, and only then would my hard work be a fragrant offering.

 So step out in faith in his strength. Study for the glory of God, and trust him with the outcome.

Train yourself to think about God in a medical context, learning about and praising God for the beauty and intricacies of his creation.

Aspects of God's character can be found throughout medicine. In the first year, students typically learn the normal functions of the human body in subjects such as anatomy, physiology, histology, and biochemistry. The amazing complexities of God's creation can serve as kindling for your sacrifice of worship. For example, if you find yourself groaning while trying to memorize the difference between the proximal and distal renal tubules, including their relative concentrating capabilities and the specific electrolytes involved, take a step back, pray, and thank God for creating the intricacies of that kidney. It is fearfully and wonderfully made (Psalm 139:14), even though it may be completely baffling to you at that moment. Transform your frustration into awe-inspired worship and praise. Study of the eye, the heart, the brain, the skin, and all of the body's other components can be spiritual tinder for worship.

Have we forgotten that God is really, really smart?

Why bring God into your studies? Because he created the human body. He knows exactly how every physiologic principle and anatomic function works. We need to ask him for wisdom in how and what to study. He isn't a decrepit great-grandfather with a mind fading into nothingness. He is the consummate physician and our great teacher

21

as well. Deliberate on his creation of his image-bearers; he knows much more than you or your professors on this subject. Work, then, with all your might, letting God's power work through you as you ask for his wisdom and strength. In the process, he will make you more like Christ in your struggles and through your victories.

Suggested Prayer

"Thank you, Lord, for calling me to use every aspect of myself—and especially my mind—to bring you glory. May I study well and lift up the time in my books as worship to you. You made all this. Help me, teach me, and guide me as I study. I am your beloved, so let me engage my studies boldly and in a way that recognizes your beauty and your elegance in creating us."

Questions to Ponder

1. Read 1 Corinthians 10:31, Matthew 22:37, Mark 12:30, and Luke 10:27. If you are meant to glorify God in all things, how does this go against the idea that studying is a secular activity to be done so that "one can then do the really godly things"?

2. If God has called you to glorify him in your studies, where does the true strength to glorify him come from?

3. When you face your books and notes this evening, what steps can you take to come before the Lord? When you are frustrated about not understanding a concept or an idea, how can Christ's love and acceptance of you be relevant in this circumstance?

4. How can understanding God's great purpose of advancing his kingdom and letting his love be made known give you better perspective when you engage yourself in medical school?

5. Take a moment to worship the awesome Creator with the course subject matter (such as renal physiology, the eye, the skin, the nervous system) that you are studying today. Do it in the midst of your studies, and keep in mind his incredible beauty, precision, and creativity.

Chapter 3 Endnotes

1. Mark A. Knoll, *The Scandal of the Evangelical Mind* (Grand Rapids, Mich.: Wm. B. Eerdmans Publishing Company, 1995), 245.
2. 1 Corinthians 14:20; John Calvin, *Concerning Scandals* (Grand Rapids, Mich.: Wm. B. Eerdmans Publishing Company, 1978), 18–19.
3. Elisabeth Elliott, *A Chance to Die, Reprinted Edition* (Grand Rapids, Mich.: Revell, 2005), 85.

CHAPTER 4

"A Time of Transitions"
by Richard Chung

During one winter break from school, I spent a few weeks traveling in eastern China. I remember going to a "foreigner's" church, where several hundred expatriates from various countries gathered to worship each Sunday. To get in, all you needed was a foreign passport to show the guard at the door, and there, amidst hundreds of like-minded brothers and sisters, you could stand and praise God in the heart of what otherwise appeared to be a spiritual ghost town.

One Sunday, the pastor asked a new couple to stand and be acknowledged by the congregation. Apparently, this couple had just arrived with plans to serve God as missionaries for seven years. Talk about a transition! While my inner voice was busy complaining about jet lag and the bitter coldness of the winter I would have to endure for the next three weeks, this husband and wife (both of whom looked to be in their forties) had packed up their belongings and placed everything in God's hands. Their transition made my "arduous" three-week sojourn look like a snip of hair at a Marine Corps barber shop, where other soldiers dove in and shaved it all off.

The couple looked wearied and frazzled, having arrived just the day before, but as we applauded and the love of Christ began to flow over them, you could see much of their worry and bewilderment melt away. God works like that. Even if a transition requires you to relinquish everything you hold dear, he will provide exactly what you need and more. In fact, in the gospel of Matthew, Christ encouraged us this way:

> Consider how the wild flowers grow. They do not labor or spin. Yet I tell you, not even Solomon in all his splendor was dressed like one of these. If that is how God clothes the grass of the field, which is here today, and tomorrow is thrown into the fire, how much more will he clothe you—you of little faith! And do not set your heart on what you will eat or drink; do not worry about it. For the pagan world runs after all such things, and your Father knows that you need them. But seek his kingdom, and these things will be given to you as well. (Luke 12:27–31)

As we make any transition in life, we may not be completely comfortable at first—or ever. God does not promise us comfort. But rest assured: if we approach his throne and his transitions with an earnest heart, he will provide all that we truly need, even as we learn, grow, and change (or stay the same), all in perfect balance.

In many ways, entering medical school is just like any other important transition in life, whether sliding through the birth canal into the bright, cold delivery room, taking those first few perilous steps, traversing puberty (ouch!), or stepping out and leaving for college. During my first year, I realized that the transition was also quite distinct in another way, as well: it was comprehensive. In addition to simply changing locations and meeting new people, I adopted a whole new language, a painfully atypical schedule, and a deeper, more nuanced perspective on humanity and the depths of our sin. Through it all, God faithfully guided me—as he will you—through the depths of this biomedical world. Although such a transition may not be what you expect or hope it to be, we know that "in all things God works for the good of those who love him" (Rom. 8:28).

Beginning medical school is only the first of many transitions that we as physicians will encounter through our training and careers, but those few words from Paul will continue to speak volumes and provide a steadying hand as we each walk through the plan that God has drawn up for our lives.

Letting Loose

A passage from the book of James also provides instruction for medical students. "Now listen, you who say, 'Today or tomorrow we will go to this or that city, spend a year there, carry on business and make money.' Why, you do not even know what will happen tomorrow. What is your life? You are a mist that appears for a little while and then vanishes. Instead, you ought to say, 'If it is the Lord's will, we will live and do this or that'" (James 4:13–15).

James focuses our eyes on God's will. As we make transitions, it is tempting to try to control all of the available parameters, foolishly believing them to be under our jurisdiction. Our understanding that God knows full well what we need for basic sustenance, both physically and spiritually, is of critical importance in unclenching our controlling hands. Our surroundings, friends, schedules, and work may all change dramatically. But our spiritual needs and our relationship with our Father in heaven remain unchanged. God knows what we need and will provide for these fundamental necessities in sufficient measure. Instead of trying to control every aspect of our transitions, it is important to let loose—almost recklessly—and dive in headlong, allowing God to pick up and arrange the pieces as he desires.

Dallas Willard, a Christian professor and philosopher, once wrote:

> What life is can only be decided as the cosmos and our understanding of it develops. The dimensions and powers of matter and life in the case of any specific type of living organism are something that can only be ascertained by bold and imaginative experimentation and observation as free from prejudgment as possible. The belief that people cannot live in constant union with the spiritual God throughout their daily li[ves] shall one day appear as odd as the belief that metal bodies cannot float on water or fly through the air. We must simply observe the living subject under all possible conditions to understand it deeply. For the matters at issue, that means that we human beings must lead our lives before God in an open, adventurous, and reflective manner. Only then shall we find what is actually possible for us as physical organisms. The wise words of Archbishop William Temple are: "We only know what matter is when spirit dwells in it; we only know what man is when God dwells in him."[1]

If you truly desire to see God establish his purpose and direction in you as you forge ahead (and as you thrust your flag into the soil of your medical education like a triumphant explorer), you need to release and let the transition take form without encumbrance. Willard points out that we can experience and enjoy the fullness of life only by observing it unfettered. Only then will we be able to see the length, width, and depth of it all. If you desire to see your life blossom in medical school, release control to God, and get ready to stand amazed.

Greener Grass

Oddly, the prototypical, American, all-you-can-eat buffet line is helpful in understanding transitions. It is quite an amazing phenomenon, actually. Aside from the methodical fasting in preparation for the buffet—and the inevitable mixed blessing of the over-satiated food coma and bloating that comes afterward—there is the phenomenon of the clean plate. Our first venture to the buffet is a little bewildering if we aren't familiar with the territory. We are not sure of the lay of the land or which foods to choose. So we try things out. There is room for trial and error. After all, once we're finished with this first plate, we simply get another and start anew. How liberating!

At this point, I've seen my friends and family go one of two ways. Some go back to what they know is good and what they enjoyed the first time around. In fact, they might go back a second time, a third time, and perhaps even a fourth. Others go in completely new directions, abandoning dishes they know to be good for the sake of variety and experimentation. I try to aim for a little of both.

I believe this is also the wisest approach as we make transitions in life. It is important for us to cherish and maintain relationships of old, lessons from the past, and habits and routines that have helped us grow, even as we dive into completely different situations with different demands on our lives and time. It is also important for us to leave much room for God to work in new and different ways, however unsettling that might be. He has brought us to each place and season in life for a reason. The places from which we depart and the places where we arrive both deserve healthy portions on our plates, because God has purposed both. Yes, I should get some more of the fried chicken if I particularly enjoyed it the first time around, but I should also leave empty space on the plate as I round the corner and explore the other side of the buffet. Who knows what I'll find? Probably something that perfectly complements my fried chicken.

Your Mission, Should You Choose to Accept It

Sitting quietly somewhere is a luxury. You can think, pray, and listen unencumbered. Take the opportunity to do exactly that before you dive into your next transition. Firmly place both hands on your relationship with God and don't let go. Hold tight to the reason God has brought you to your current path, and anchor it in your mind and heart. Allow it to become a familiar navigational beacon. First, center yourself on what truly matters; then let loose.

Before entering the world of your new school and the broader galaxy of medicine, make every effort to concretize in your heart and soul the purpose God has given you in your study and future practice of medicine. He has brought you to the brink of an amazing experience of growth and learning for very specific reasons. Perhaps not all of them are clear just yet, but it is important to understand that they exist, nonetheless. Although our personal plans typically look one day, one week, or—if we're particularly ambitious—one month into the future, God's plans span eternity. Nothing in your transition is a surprise to God. Centering yourself upon that understanding will help immensely in keeping you focused and alert as you take those first few steps.

From day one, your school and any vague concept you may have of medicine will ceaselessly try to convince you to settle for the "good enough" reasons to learn medicine, but not the best reason. It is good to help people with their struggles. It is good to accrue new knowledge. It is good to help lessen pain and discomfort. But even those who don't know Christ can claim those motivations. As Christians, Christ's glory alone is the reason we do anything.

Holding firm to that fundamental truth will help guide every other aspect of your transition, and you will find that the worries and concerns you used to pore over compulsively will fall into place behind the flagship of your faith.

God's will for you in medicine is the only guidepost you need. Like a trusty compass, it will prove both beautifully simple and comfortingly clear in the midst of what oftentimes feels like incredible chaos. God and his glory are your mission. Please accept the mission, and don't get sidetracked.

Suggested Prayer

"Lord, I know that many things change with time. I pray that as I begin this transition into medical school, I would remember that you do not promise comfort and ease, but you do promise to give me everything I need to live a godly life. Give me courage to go forth in your strength, trusting in you. Remind me that even though I may not know what lies ahead, nothing escapes your purpose for my life. Help me to go confidently in your name. Give me strength to adjust to this new environment and the people you put before me. May Christ's glory be my heart's desire for everything I encounter and do today."

Questions to Ponder

1. What sorts of transitions (geographical or personal) have you experienced in your life? As you were facing each one, how did you feel about it?
2. How did you go about preparing for those transitions? How did God factor into your preparation (if at all)?

3. Think about the statement, "First, center yourself on what truly matters; then let loose." What does this mean as you transition into medical school?
4. How does making your primary motivation to glorify God guide specific aspects of your transition?

Chapter 4 Endnotes

1. Dallas Willard, *Spirit of the Disciplines* (New York: HarperOne, 1990), 78.

CHAPTER 5

"86,400 Seconds" by Richard Chung

There are 86,400 seconds in every twenty-four hours. It certainly seems like a lot, yet many medical students and doctors alike wouldn't mind twenty-five or even twenty-six hours in a day (unless they were on call!). Considering the amount of time we spend sleeping, eating, commuting, and doing a whole host of other seemingly "unproductive" things, coupled with our propensity as medical professionals to overload ourselves with work and commitments, it is not surprising that time is always lacking. It is also not surprising that many eternally productive activities, such as studying the Bible and prayer, are often relegated to the imaginary twenty-fifth and twenty-sixth hours of each day.

Medical school holds a lofty position in academia as a unique time of inordinate rigor in terms of both our studies and the physical demands upon our bodies. It wasn't designed to fit into neat little twenty-four-hour packages. Like the struggle to fit into jeans that are two or three sizes too small, the impassioned drive to make all of our activities fit into twenty-four hours will not only ultimately prove futile, but it will be enormously frustrating and painful.

One quote (commonly attributed to C. S. Lewis) puts it bluntly: "Time hasn't stopped for any troubles, heartaches, or any other malfunctions of this world, so please don't tell me it will stop for you." The author is right. The onslaught of time characterizes much of medical school and the training that follows it. Time truly flies, and there is just so much to do. But remember that God created time, so who better to turn to for help in managing it?

So Much to Do, So Little Time

When I go to the grocery store after having skipped lunch, suddenly everything on the shelves looks appetizing, and I find my cart overloaded with junk food. I've picked up the essentials, to be sure, but I have also ravenously invited cheese doodles, fudge-striped wafer cookies, and a couple pints of the purple stuff along for the ride. On most days, I'll come to my senses prior to checking out and put most of it back, but in order to know how best to do this, I need to prioritize.

So it is with time. As you meticulously write out a weekly schedule and attempt to budget your time, it is helpful to write out a list of your key priorities, as well as every cheese doodle, carton of eggs, and loaf of Wonder Bread that makes its claim on your time. Only with this list in hand will you be prepared to approach the checkout line and see how far your wallet of time will take you.

Making Your List and Checking It Twice

Your list of priorities speaks volumes, not only about what is important to you, but also about your understanding of your core purpose in medical school. If your time with God begins to get squeezed out, stop everything—at all costs—and refocus, even if it takes several seconds or minutes away from your studies. When your hunger to conquer certain topics of medicine (diabetes, the brachial plexus, the

Krebs cycle) begins to edge out your hunger for the truths and lessons of God, stop everything and refocus. When you begin to relish your time hunched over a microscope or a cadaver more than you relish your time hunched over in prayer, stop everything and refocus.

I've found the encroachment of medicine upon my time to be ceaseless. Because these moments of conflict between my finite time and my infinite to-do list are so frequent and difficult to navigate, it is immensely important for me to use the word "nonnegotiable" as I parse through my list. I've found this word to be indispensable, and I recommend that you add it to your everyday vocabulary. Try it; it has a certain sweet and firm ring to it. Nonnegotiables are stubborn and inflexible claims on your time. They are both irresistible forces and immovable objects at the same time.

For me, I found that certain things had to be black-and-white, because if there was even one exception in which I subordinated a nonnegotiable, it was the push of medicine. In the operating room, blue drapes need to be complete, without holes or "exceptions" to the aseptic rule to which they relate. If there is even one small hole at the far end of the surgical field, the principle of sterility and aseptic technique is compromised. So should be our nonnegotiables. We can't afford to fool ourselves, because there are certain things that are just that important. Your spiritual health is one of them. The ramifications of compromising it are disastrous.

Testing Your Reflexes

As you sit down to figure out your nonnegotiables—if you are anything like I was early on in medical school—studying will probably nudge its way to the very top of your list. Don't let it. At all costs, keep it tamed! Studying is, of course, enormously important and a key aspect of stewarding the educational opportunity with which God has blessed you. But the line between being a good steward and performing a hostile takeover can be subtle and, in your eyes, nebulously shifting. Keep looking for that line, and remain conscious of it. The slope on the other side is not just slippery but destructively sweet and falsely satisfying.

Ratcheting your academics to the top of your list is natural and reflexive, because you are a student. You were admitted to medical school because you fared well in college. Your will to try hard and do well most likely has defined a large chunk of who you believe yourself to be. It certainly did for me. The inevitable spirit of competition that came with medical school took those hardworking instincts and amplified them. When the pressure increased, I instinctively worked harder, until some modicum of success told me that I could relax just a little bit. How quickly I turned to my own abilities to stay afloat, while forgetting that God had generously granted me the opportunities to attend medical school in the first place! J. I. Packer wrote:

> We are not persuaded of the adequacy of God to provide for all the ends of those who launch out wholeheartedly on the deep sea of unconventional living in obedience to the call of Christ. Therefore, we feel obliged to break the first commandment just a little, by withdrawing a certain amount of our time and energy from serving God in order to serve mammon. This, at bottom, seems to be what is wrong with us. We are afraid to go all the way in accepting the authority of God, because of our secret uncertainty as to his adequacy to look after us if we do.[1]

Prioritizing God above medicine—or anything for that matter—is truly unconventional living. Yet, as Packer notes, we don't trust him quite enough. Oh, pesky mammon! This is why wholehearted obedience to Christ must be our heart's unconditional commitment.

All Time Is Not Equal

After establishing my nonnegotiables, I came to realize that the value of my time was not the same at every hour of the day. Unlike money, where every US dollar bill has equal value, the value of minutes varies dramatically, based on the time of day. For me, one minute during the 11:00 a.m. hour was much more productive than an identical chunk at 12:34 a.m. It was essential for me to understand this before bringing my time to God's throne as an offering.

In 2 Samuel 24, King David declared, "I will not sacrifice to the Lord my God burnt offerings that cost me nothing." This was in response to Araunah the Jebusite's offer to provide a threshing floor, oxen, and other necessities, free of charge, as David prepared a burnt offering to the Lord. David refused the offer and insisted on paying for it all. David understood that God doesn't simply desire something—*anything*. God desires and delights in costly offerings and costly worship. The same goes for your time. As you carefully prioritize and budget your time, you need to prorate the value of each minute accurately and only then bring your time to the Lord.

Although it is not widely realized, with God it is possible to create more time. No, God does not stop or slow time for the benefit of certain people. Nor does he add seconds or hours here and there (except for leap years!). Instead, he effectively increases the time you have each day by increasing your efficiency. Remaining focused on him will sustain your calm in struggle, clear your mind in chaos, and give you renewed strength and resolve in the midst of exhaustion.

Cutting God out doesn't give you an extra fifteen or twenty minutes in the day. It effectively subtracts productive time from it. Martin Luther once wrote, "I have so much business I cannot get on without spending three hours daily in prayer."[2] Contrary to most of our instincts, busyness and the lack of sufficient time were what drove Luther to take even more time to pray. He realized the primacy of God in all things, and therefore he knew that the busier he was, the wiser it was to spend even more time with the Creator of time. If we center ourselves on God throughout the day, we will feel as if we've finally discovered the twenty-fifth or twenty-sixth hour.

Make Everything Count

Finally, and perhaps most importantly, I learned that it was critical to make everything in my day count for God. Paul wrote, "Whether you eat or drink or whatever you do, do it all for the glory of God" (1 Cor. 10:31). Although we have discussed carving out specific times for God and specific times for studying and other pursuits, practically and biblically, God wants it all.

Over time, I realized that God wanted not just a discrete appointment with me, but the entirety of my day. After making my list, choosing my priorities, and scheduling my activities, I needed to take my God-sections and "smear" them throughout every other section. Every activity of every day needed to be colored by my relationship with God. Everything in medical school needed to be colored by the overarching purpose that God had given me. After everything was said and done, I was in medical school to demonstrate God's love and compassion and to minister effectively to those around me, whether they were patients, fellow students, or even the dean of the faculty.

By constantly reflecting on each activity and trying to perceive whether God was guiding my hand, I was able to work toward keeping my life allegiant to God and maximize my productivity, not just in terms of earthly metrics but in terms of eternal worth. As you press onward, if you keep God at the forefront, twenty-four hours can become a blessed eternity, and your work will always be complete by the time you lay your head down.

Suggested Prayer

"Father, sometimes I feel that there is so much to do and so little time to do it. Please help me prioritize my nonnegotiables and do those things first. Please pull me back if I start getting carried away by all the things I 'need' to get done. I give you my firstfruits, Lord. I know that this sacrifice is nothing compared to what your Son has done for me in giving me new life and eternal hope. When I wake up in the mornings, fill me with your presence and power. When I lie down at the end of the day, forgive my mess-ups. Above all, Lord, let your redemptive work be done in and through me, and let everything I do in the twenty-four hours you have given me be done for your glory."

Questions to Ponder

1. Write out a list of what you do on a typical weekday. Prioritize your activities in order of importance and identify the nonnegotiables. With the command to give God your firstfruits, is there room for restructuring your day?
2. With question one in mind, is there a way you can be more efficient so that you can also find time to bring rest for your mind and soul?
3. How can you "smear" your God-appointed times throughout every other part of the day?

Chapter 5 Endnotes

1. J. I. Packer, *Knowing God* (Downers Grove, Ill.: InterVarsity Press, 1973), 270.

2. Richard J. Foster, *Celebration of Discipline* (New York: Harper Collins, 1988), 34.

CHAPTER 6

Medical School as a Foreign Language and Culture

Have you ever been to a place where the language and culture is so different that you were helpless without the aid of someone who knew the area or the people? I had that experience many years ago when I traveled with my family to Japan. The weeklong tour offered fully prepared Japanese meals, impeccably clean hotels, and a bus that shuttled us comfortably from place to place. We explored Tokyo and its surrounding areas and met its residents, which was an incredible experience.

However, as much as I enjoyed the five-star treatment, we never felt truly at-home because we were strangers (albeit pampered ones) in a foreign land. If I had a question while shopping, all I could do was point to an item I was interested in and repeat myself over and over again—of course, to little effect! As warmly received as I was, the barriers of language and culture kept me from truly connecting in a deeply meaningful way with the Japanese people.

In our medical training, we find ourselves in a place of unfamiliarity as well. We are thrown into medicine and are expected to learn its language and culture in a short time. Technical terms like *myelomeningocele, Wolf-Parkinson-White syndrome, prosopagnosia,* and a lengthy supply of acronyms flood our brains daily. We are expected not only to speak fluently in this jargon but to describe it in understandable terms to the patients we care for. (Imagine, for example, explaining *thrombotic thrombocytopenic purpura* to a friend who doesn't have a medical background.) In the midst of it all, we are also learning how to interact professionally with our attendings, residents, and patients.

This could be a daunting task, and sometimes it got the better of me. Whenever I felt overwhelmed, I reminisced about "those good ol' days in college," when there had been ample time for fellowship with good friends, not to mention the extralong breaks between classes to enjoy meals with them! Those were the days when it had been easy to worship God. And wasn't that what really mattered? What was I doing, throwing myself into this desert environment that took my time from God and drained me dry of fellowship with others? I wondered if the Bible had anything good to say about stepping into and charting a course in a foreign land like this eccentric culture of medicine. Not surprisingly, it did.

The Lord's Approval of Learning

A few thousand years ago, one student of culture, Daniel of Judah, experienced something similar. Daniel had been placed under the rule of the reigning king of Babylon, Nebuchadnezzar, to serve in the king's palace. Of the Israelites there, Daniel and his friends were among those chosen by the king to be taught the language and literature of the land. As you read through the book of Daniel, it is crucial to realize that throughout his life, Daniel did not think of studying about and learning of Babylon as anti-God. Nor did he think that his academic endeavors kept him from worshipping God. On the contrary, "to these four young men God gave knowledge and understanding of all kinds of literature and learning" (Dan. 1:17).

God thought it was important enough to give Daniel and his friends the knowledge and ability to understand the Babylonian culture they were living in. God was directly invested in their everyday lives, not just the sweet by-and-by.

When I first realized that God had a vested interested in Daniel's studies, I was shocked. All the time I'd spent missing great fellowship from my college days, I had actually been missing the heart of God for me in learning the language and literature of the "fellowship" of medicine. Daniel didn't pine after the good old days of Jerusalem, moping that his land had been taken over by the Babylonian king. He focused on his new environment and made a purposeful decision to glorify God in it. In the same way, I needed to focus myself in this new world of medicine and to honor God in the midst of it.

Look to the One Who Blesses

Daniel approached his new world with the knowledge that the Lord was walking with him, approving of and empowering him in his studies. Daniel and his friends were given a level of understanding that impressed even the king: "He found none equal to Daniel and his friends Hananiah, Mishael and Azariah; so they entered the king's service. In every matter of wisdom and understanding about which the king questioned them, he found them ten times better than all the magicians and enchanters in his whole kingdom" (Dan. 1:18–20). In the same way, you must look to the Lord to empower your studying of medicine, realizing that he brought you to this world and wants you to succeed by honoring him in your medical education.

Daniel was immensely blessed as he grew in stature and recognition in Babylon. But honoring the Lord was no guarantee of worldly success, and Daniel knew that. His consistent response was one of faith in the Lord, regardless of the cost. As a teenager, he refused to eat the king's food (at risk to his life) to keep from defiling himself before God. And he continued praying to God, even under threat of being thrown into the lion's den.

Similarly, when his friends, Shadrach, Meshach, and Abednego stood on trial before the king for refusing to bow before other gods, they did not know whether their lives would be spared or whether they would be burned to death: "If we are thrown into the blazing furnace, the God we serve is able to save us from it, and he will rescue us from your hand, O King. But even if he does not, we want to you to know, O King, that we will not serve your gods or worship the image of gold you have set up" (Dan. 3:17–18). What steadfast faith!

Their ultimate goal was not prosperity or high socioeconomic standing, even though their positions primed them for it. They still chose faithfulness, even when threatened with death. Their desire was simply to honor God. We know how the amazing story unfolds: King Nebuchadnezzar threw Daniel's three friends into the blazing furnace, but instead of being burned alive, they were preserved by God. This miracle moved the king so deeply that he promoted the three to positions of even greater influence for God's kingdom.

During my first year of medical school, I realized that if my goal was to honor God, then I had to honor him in the process of reaching that goal. When I found myself nearing burnout—after presenting a case to an attending, or memorizing the nerves of the lumbosacral plexus or the multiple steps of the coagulation cascade—I would take a deep breath and remind myself that I was in the process of learning the language and literature of this "country" in which God had placed me.

Likewise, as you learn the language and experience the culture of medicine, remember to follow Daniel's example by asking God to give you the knowledge and ability to understand what you are studying. Your aim should be neither to do the bare minimum to get by nor to sacrifice everything in order to be the superstar in your class. We will discuss how this works more specifically in the next chapter.

In the meantime, let your one goal be to honor and worship the Lord. God is watching over you and will sustain you through these times. Like Daniel, Shadrach, Meshach, and Abednego, if you entrust yourself to him, the opportunities to give God glory in the midst of the fire of your circumstances may be even greater than you realize.

Suggested Prayer

"Lord, thank you that Daniel and his three faithful friends can be an example of faith for me. Help me remember that it is you who blessed them with the knowledge and understanding of Babylon's culture. You also have called me to this place of medicine, with its own unique language and culture. Bless my studies as well. I pray that, like those young men, I would honor you in my situation, regardless of the outcome. Give me the courage to stand up to any compromise that keeps me from being a blessing to you. Give me the conviction, integrity, and character to honor you, no matter how fiery the trials might become. Be glorified in all I say and do."

Questions to Ponder

1. Have you ever traveled to a place in which the culture was foreign to you? If so, what things, people, or experiences made you feel out-of-place, and what made you feel more at-home?
2. What was Daniel's response to being placed in a new environment and being required to learn the language and

literature of the Babylonian Empire? How can that help you in your approach to this new culture of medical school?

3. Do you think that honoring the Lord guarantees academic success: top honors in your class or being part of the national honor society, Alpha Omega Alpha (AOA), and so on? What was Daniel's perspective?

4. What was Daniel's overarching desire as he grew in stature and recognition in Babylon? How do we know this?

5. How does Daniel's example encourage us to make honoring God the focus of our lives in this new culture of medicine in which we now live?[1]

Chapter 6 Endnotes

1. For further study in the book of Daniel as it relates to your medical training, pick up the Bible study, *Living in the Lab without Smelling Like a Cadaver* by William Peel, published by CMDA, December 1999.

CHAPTER 7

You Versus the Competition: How Far Will You Go?

One afternoon during my pediatric rotation, I saw an exam room door fling open and a nurse come staggering out: "I can't control them! They're too strong!" As the nurse stumbled past us, the doctor and I gave each other a quizzical look. She was talking about the two-year-old twins she was trying to work up before we saw them.

We gathered our charts, entered the room, and saw the mom hunched over, pinning one of the twins between her legs, while trying to comfort the other on the exam table. Both were squirming and screaming but in good spirits. As the mother turned around to face me, I froze in a split-second of shock.

The whites of both her eyes were a deep scarlet red—not the usual I-have-allergies red or even the my-eyes-are-bloodshot-because-I-stayed-up-last-night red, but a color that looked as if someone had taken dark, blood-red paint and smeared her eyes with it (in medical terminology, a *subconjunctival hemorrhage*). She was in her early thirties but with a face so tired that she looked to be in her late forties.

The pediatrician examined each child's eyes and ears by holding the head, while I grasped the arms and the mom kept the rest of the body from moving. The twins were fighters! Suddenly the mom put her hand on mine, and with a worried tone in her voice said, "Oh, please don't hurt them." Though my grip on them wasn't tight, I let go ever-so-slightly.

I found out later that the father of her twins not only wasn't paying child support but was the perpetrator of those blood-red eyes. He had choked the mother so fiercely that the vessels in her eyes had burst and bled. It was no wonder that she had an instinctive reaction to protect her children. When the pediatrician gently pressed her about it, she looked down and replied, "I can handle it. No, I don't want to press charges."

The pediatrician was obligated to report it, and I don't know the outcome of her situation, but the more I thought I about it, the more I realized how tragically ironic it was. Here was a mother telling me not to hurt her children as I was trying to help them, while she continued living with the one who had strangled her to point where her eyes hemorrhaged. But before I could shake my head and say, "Why do people let these things happen to themselves?," I had to ask myself what I was willing to sacrifice when I really wanted something. If I wanted something badly enough, wouldn't I do almost anything to get it? If I desired it at any cost, would I be willing to give up my own dignity, self-respect, or integrity to obtain it?

How about you? What are you willing to give up for what you really, really want—that grade, that residency program, that collegial recognition, that prestigious grant?

There is no doubt that it takes academic ability to get into medical school. Therefore, you will likely find that your peers are at least on-par with you intellectually. Perhaps they are even more gifted than you are. While you may have been among the top performers in your college class, you may now find yourself smack-dab in the middle of the bell curve. That transition can lead to unhealthy comparisons and competition that can be destructive to your life.

Teddy, a first-year medical student, shared with me that he found it difficult to study excellently without "gunning it," meaning waylaying everything in his path to get the top score in class, whether it be sleep, friends, a pleasant disposition, or even his sanity. He admitted that he was beginning to feel the pressure of wanting to stack his resume with grades, extracurricular activities, and so on. His concerns echoed the same ones I too had faced. Should I be satisfied with "just passing"? How hard should I try for honors? How was I to study for the Lord in an excellent way without "gunning" it—that is, sacrificing my soul—in the process?

It is good to maximize your knowledge in the pursuit of becoming an excellent doctor, but unless your medical school has only a pass/fail grading system, there will inevitably be competition. Although we should take pleasure and satisfaction in knowing that we've learned something well, there are times we feel that inner urge to glance over at our classmate's paper or exam to see just how well we did in comparison. *Just how good was my grade or boards score? Am I in the top or bottom of the class?* That temptation can be hard to resist! We think the score itself is not enough to tell us how well we've done. We want to know how we did in comparison to others.

What's more, if we have done exceptionally well, it is hard to avoid being smug—not out loud, most likely, because that isn't the Christian thing to do—but our hearts can swell with deceptive arrogance, thinking that our worth has somehow been validated by virtue of performing better than our peers. If we do poorly, we can have the opposite reaction as well, and it would be equally wrong. That same pride that lets us lord it over others also makes us ashamed when we are doing poorly. We berate ourselves: "Why were my college classes such a breeze, and now I just can't seem to cut it? I feel like an idiot.

I can't keep up with everyone else. They all seem to get it, but for me there is too much information and not enough time."

It was immensely important for me to realize that both reactions— selfish conceit and self-loathing—were dreadfully wrong. Just as self-righteous boasting did not glorify the one who gave me talents in the first place, neither did self-denigration, which denied the value God bestowed upon me as his loved and forgiven child. Comparing yourself to others in order to determine your self-worth is a subtle but extremely dangerous thing to do, because it factors out the only true way you should look at your life: from God's perspective. Romans 12:3 (MSG) states it well: "The only accurate way to understand ourselves is by what God is and by what he does for us, not by what we are and what we do for him."

Struggling through medical school is normal. There may be some things you just "get" easily and other things you have to spend much more time on. More than just having a healthy expectation and respect for the challenges of medicine, understand that your value is not grounded in your performance. Fight the temptation to base your self-worth on how well or poorly you do on your exams, especially when it comes to comparing your evaluations or scores to those of others. Trust in God's all-surpassing love and grace for you, and know that you are called to a profession that asks you to do your best in the fullness of strength only he can provide.

Dr. Harvey Elder, a wonderful, godly physician I met on a summer medical missions project, approaches the subject of studying for the glory of God by first understanding our calling as medical students. In a letter to me, he wrote:

> The issue is not "gunning it" but stewardship—that is, care for all that God has entrusted to us.

While [those who "gun" it] may have a … higher score, their ability to retain information will be limited. They will be less able to put what they know into practice. They will exhaust themselves fighting their fear of "failure." They will strive for recognition and fear punishment (not getting the top grade, not getting the pristine house officer training and thus not accomplishing their goal). All of these are disabling and distracting. In the end, three to seven years out of medicine (i.e., after residency), the steward of God's call will be far more effective by any metric and much better prepared to continue in obedience to God's call on his/her life.

Any student can increase his grade point average to some extent by pressing his mental capacities to their limits at the expense of the other dimensions of personhood. The reasons for doing so could be found in the student's value system. If the value system accepts the popular economy that power, wealth, and/or academic standing are the goals, then pushing the mental at the expense of all else makes some sort of sense. If, however, the person's value system says, "Obedience to God's call is my goal," then acknowledgment of God's concern for the entirety of one's person would lead to caring for oneself in those terms.[1]

Take a Break—A Good One

As you take care of your physical, mental, emotional, and spiritual life, remember the value of rest and renewal. This means getting away from your daily stresses and spending time on things you enjoy and that bring you refreshment.

In an article called "Defining Life Backwards," Ravi Zacharias spoke wisely about rest and pleasure when he said, "[T]here is a fundamental prerequisite for defining any legitimate pleasure in life and that is to first establish the purpose of life itself. All pleasure is built upon why you and I exist in the first place."[2] As you make efforts to find rest from your studies (which you should do on a regular basis), consider this insightful principle: "Any pleasure that refreshes you without diminishing you, distracting you, or sidetracking you from the ultimate goal is a legitimate pleasure."[3]

I found relief in intramural volleyball during the fall and spring seasons. I found it not only a good time to let go of unspent stress, but also a great time to meet other people who weren't in medical school. It let me realize that there was still a world outside the bubble of medicine, and that on occasion I could go outside of it and breathe some fresh air. Others I knew spent time in the arts that pointed toward the beauty of God, whether it was visiting a museum, watching a musical, or creating their own beauty through painting, sculpting, or knitting.

Find refreshment in the things you enjoy. Eric Liddell, the 1924 Summer Olympic Games gold-medalist runner portrayed in the classic movie *Chariots of Fire* (1981) stated, "I believe God made me for a purpose, but he also made me fast. And when I run, I feel his pleasure." As you take part in your opportunities for refreshment, may you also feel God's pleasure and be renewed through it!

If you have established in your heart that you are loved and valued by God and that his will for you matters more than how much better (or worse) you did than your classmates, you will bring God glory in every aspect of your life, during your academic studies and your times of rest. Jesus calls you first and foremost to desire him, not to seek comparison of how you have fared in relation to others. May you find your wholeness in the one who is the Creator and fulfillment of such desire.

Suggested Prayer

"Father, I pray that I would not let how well or how poorly I do in class affect the way I view myself. Let me be guided by the bigger reality that the only way to have a true perspective on myself is to see how you see me. Thank you that you died for me. Thank you that I am now your beloved. Thank you that I can study without the need to compare myself to others in order to feel worthy or validated. I pray that you would strengthen me and give me the wisdom and power to see that obedience to you is my ultimate goal and primary calling in life. May I be a true steward of the intellect, energy, and time with which you have blessed me. Be glorified when I study, and may you grant me true spiritual refreshment in my times of rest."

Questions to Ponder

1. Describe a situation, either in medical school or in your past, in which you felt you just had to have something, and the lengths you took to get it.
2. When you receive a test score, what is the first thing you think of—how you could have done better, how well you did in comparison to others, or something else? Is it okay to compare your scores with those of others? When can it be a stumbling block and detrimental to your faith?
3. Why is basing your self-worth on how well you do compared to others an unhealthy spiritual misconception?
4. How can you take to heart the truth that "obedience to God's call is your goal" and not push your mental capacities

to the limit at the expense of all other things for the sake of academic success?

5. In which activities or people can you find true rest and enjoyment that, as Ravi Zacharias says, will refresh you "without diminishing you, distracting you, or sidetracking you from the ultimate goal"? Deliberately factor these times of purposeful refreshment into your schedule.

Chapter 7 Endnotes

1. Dr. Harvey Elder, personal communication.
2. Ravi Zacharias, "Defining Life Backwards," *A Slice of Infinity*, 3-27-2000.
3. Ibid.

CHAPTER 8

Divine Fellowship:
The Christian Community

My first year of medical school was an exciting time of meeting new friends, studying furiously, and learning the building blocks of medicine. However, the experience lacked visible Christians, myself included. There were no structured Christian organizations or societies at the time, and since no one in our class was an outspoken believer, it was not easy to tell who was a Christian just by looking around. I attended church on Sundays, but I did not make much effort to be spiritually challenged, let alone try to challenge and encourage others.

That year, I realized that a Lone Ranger approach—learning medicine without the fellowship of other Christians—resulted in a weakening desire to live for Christ and a strengthened desire to live for self. I studied so that people would look up to me (whenever I did well, that is), hoping for the satisfaction of labeling myself as the cream of the crop from an Ivy League medical school. Even more, I studied out of fear that my classmates would see me as incompetent or—compared to them—just plain dumb. Inherently bound up in that fear was the belief that my standing in class meant more than my standing before God. The pressure to do well (whether real or imagined) was especially heightened during times of stress. It was too easy to get caught up in the flow of what everyone else was thinking and doing.

The temptation to compare ourselves with others is a result of our own spiritual blindness. In Matthew 7:3–5, Jesus spoke very strongly about this temptation. He said, "Why do you look at the speck of sawdust in your brother's eye and pay no attention to the plank in your own eye? How can you say to your brother, 'Let me take the speck out of your eye,' when all the time there is a plank in your own eye?"

As a result of our blindness, we can deceive ourselves into believing that we are doing all right spiritually, despite signs to the contrary. We might ask ourselves, "Why should I make an effort to fellowship with other believers? I go to church on Sundays. Isn't that good enough? They should be glad I even go! I'm too busy to spend time doing anything other than studying anyway." Others may struggle with the fact that there are very few Christians in their schools, and of those, many halfheartedly pay their respects to God by trying not to complain and being "the cheerful Christian I'm supposed to be." Attitudes like these actually reveal a serious misunderstanding of God's call for the fellowship and unity of all believers.

We need others to make sure our hearts stay in tune with God's, because we underestimate the level to which we can be masters of self-deception. The writer of Hebrews makes this point: "See to it, brothers, that none of you has a sinful, unbelieving heart that turns away from the living God. But encourage one another daily, as long as it is called 'Today,' so that none of you may be hardened by sin's deceitfulness" (Heb. 3:12–13). Christ has broken the power of sin, but like a nagging, persistent cough, the presence of sin remains. Our hearts are still prone to being hardened by our personal weaknesses and our difficult circumstances. No person can thrive spiritually over the long haul apart from a community of believers. Such people are like cut flowers. They may look good and thrive for a little while, but eventually they will wilt.

Understanding the biblical mandate for the believer to be part of the church body is essential in establishing a scripturally grounded motivation for communing with God's family. Dietrich Bonhoeffer said,

> God has willed that we should seek and find His living Word in the witness of brothers, in the mouth of man. Therefore, the Christian needs another Christian who speaks God's Word to him. He needs him again and again when he becomes uncertain and discouraged, for by himself he cannot help himself without belying the truth. He needs his brother man as a bearer and proclaimer of the divine word of salvation. He needs his brother solely because of Jesus Christ. The Christ in his own heart is weaker than the Christ in the word of his brother; his own heart is uncertain, his brother's is sure.[1]

We need others to reveal the Word of God to us in order to get an accurate picture of who we are. We need to encourage one another so that we will not be hardened and turn away from God by the deceitfulness of our sin.

What Does Fellowship Entail?

"It is not the healthy who need a doctor, but the sick. I have not come to call the righteous, but sinners" (Mark 2:17).

David, a good friend of mine, made an interesting point while we were milling about one night after a large group fellowship. He said, "You know, I've noticed that oftentimes a 'law of reversal' takes place when we are feeling down in the dumps. It's at that very time when we really want to connect with people, but because of some kind of negative aura we give off, everyone somehow ends up avoiding us." I had to agree with him. Doesn't it seem as if people tend to gravitate toward the outgoing, everything–is–going–really–well kind of person? It is often the person who most needs that kind word, gentle touch, or listening ear who is most easily passed by.

This is very much in keeping with our selfish nature. I have felt the pressure of having to appear "put-together" before both my believing and nonbelieving peers. Often the fruit of selfish pride gets expressed in competitive remarks or thoughts: "What? You don't know at least eight differential diagnoses for clubbing of the fingers? Come on! Basic stuff!" Fellowship is not for meeting together to let others know how well put-together we are. Nor is it to fulfill a quota of spiritual good deeds. There were many times when I didn't feel like leaving my apartment, because at home I was in my comfort zone. Why did I have to put on a public facade that I had everything together when I was actually very broken? It was so hard to meet new people, especially at church. I spent almost all my "people time" in the hospital, seeing patients, and it became strange to talk to people just to be friendly. I felt like a social barbarian, able to interact with people, but not really able to grow in my social character, especially as it related to the church body.

Ephesians 1:23 says that the church "is his body, the fullness of him who fills everything in every way." God may have given each one of us an individual calling, but he has not called any of us to be individualistic in our living. Paul exhorted us to "speak to one another with psalms, hymns and songs from the Spirit" (Eph. 5:19) and to encourage one another with words that "build each other up according to their needs, that it may benefit those who listen" (Eph. 4:29). This means we are to speak gospel truths to each other. If we don't, our wandering hearts will quickly forget the meaningful blessing of fellowship and believe the lie that spending time with other believers is a waste of our time.

Just as Paul instructed the Ephesian church to encourage one another in the body of Christ, we also should be deliberate in the way we fellowship with one another. What does this action look like? Paul Tripp says, "We need the loving courage of honesty and the thankful humility of approachability. We need to love others more than we love ourselves, and so, with humble, patient love, help them to see what they need to see … we need to forsake defensiveness [and] be thankful that God has surrounded us with help, and be ready to receive it—every day!"[2]

The body of believers is a place where we come to pray and voice our struggles, fears, and frustrations. As we begin to establish ourselves in community, we begin to see a relationship, as Alan Medinger says, "in which a Christian gives permission to another believer to look into his life for purposes of questioning, challenging, admonishing, advising, encouraging, and otherwise providing input in ways that will help the individual live according to the Christian principles that they both hold."[3]

Ponder the words of the writer of Hebrews: "Let us consider how we may spur one another on toward love and good deeds. Let us not give up meeting together, as some are in the habit of doing, but let us encourage one another—and all the more as you see the Day approaching" (Heb. 10:24–25).

After a year of trying the Lone Ranger approach, I knew that something wasn't right. Like walking with only one shoe on, I felt unbalanced. The Holy Spirit, however, still persisted: "Eric, there is another way to approach this." In the midst of everything, I threw up a desperate prayer for some form of accountability, even someone just to listen to what I was dealing with. Well, the Lord provided. Not too long afterward, a dermatology resident I had met at a church fellowship offered to meet up and pray with me every week. Though our meetings consisted of me doing most of the talking (and complaining), I treasured those times of sharing my fears and struggles and was encouraged that he took the time simply to listen to what I had to say and to pray for me.

Whenever I felt the temptation to study so I could establish some sort of hierarchy over my peers, my new prayer partner reminded me that I really was studying for just one Master, the Lord, and doing it for his glory alone. When I complained about how trying it was to learn every last detail in histology class, he encouraged me to sit back, pause for a moment, and just marvel at the intricacies of the human body (which God, in his magnificent wisdom, created), while praying, "The complexity and amount of information is sometimes beyond me, Lord, but I praise you that you made each and every system, organ, and protein, for you are the Creator of all good things, and you are wonderfully mind-blowing! Please help me understand more about this awesome creation you've made in us."

My friend's presence comforted me. In him, I knew that there was someone who wanted to honor God, and thinking of him whenever I felt discouraged helped me realize that, with a community of believers, my faith could truly grow. You too can grow in the Lord, even in medical school! In fact, you have a unique opportunity to reflect God to other believers and to your colleagues. Here are three suggestions for how to be that kind of God-glorifying presence.

Remind each other why you do what you do.

Colossians 3:17 tells us that "whatever you do, whether in word or deed, do it all in the name of the Lord Jesus, giving thanks to God the Father through him." Christian doctors are called to serve in a variety of settings, from suburbia to the remotest jungles, but for now, an important part of your calling is to be just what you are: a medical student. The Creator of the human body (which you are now studying) brought you to where you are by his sovereign choice.

Choose to live thankfully and serve him faithfully where you are at this very moment.

Remind each other that studying God's creation is an opportunity to worship him.

Medical school offers a window into the creativity and love of God by virtue of his design of the human body. It is very easy to roll your eyes and grumble under the enormous weight of information being taught. Instead of seeing that enormous corpus of information as simply data to be memorized, try leaning toward God with a mind that seeks a deeper understanding of his deliberate purpose in creating humankind in his own image. We were designed by our Creator, so worship and give thanks to him for making us so intricately functional and beautiful.

Remind each other that Christian community provides an alternate outlook to the culture of medicine, particularly when we suffer for the sake of the gospel.

The path of learning medicine is at times painful and fraught with suffering, but it is also marked with deep joy and worship of God in a way that is unique to the medical experience. Medical education is often malignant (studies have shown that 30 percent or more of medical students struggle with burnout or depression during their training[4]), but the community of believers can offer the downtrodden a healthier and more encouraging outlook, giving strength to sustain them through the stress and strain of medical student life.

The Christian Medical and Dental Associations (CMDA), for example, is on 92 percent of the medical school campuses in the United States and provides opportunities where fellow Christians students can gather, encourage, and grow together. Go to www. cmda.org and click under the "Students" section to find out what events are going on and who to contact on your campus. And if you are unable to attend services on Sunday morning, find a local church that offers a service at a different time or day, or consider joining a community group that is part of that church.

The importance of fellowship among medical students or with a believing mentor—in medicine or in the church—should not be underestimated. Be comforted that, whatever your situation, whether you are part of a thriving fellowship or the only believer in your class, God desires your spiritual growth in a community. He will provide opportunities for you as you come to him and participate in being healed, restored, and encouraged by his people, his church.

Suggested Prayer

"Father, I confess that it is so easy to just want to do things on my own. Even with my Christian walk, I feel as if I can survive on my own. But I know that is not how you made things to be. I confess that my heart is deceitful above all things, and because of this, I need others to encourage me and help me keep my eyes focused upon you. Your Word has called and commanded me to worship you with a community of believers. I pray that you would provide for me a community that loves Jesus. I pray you would help me connect in a deeply meaningful and consistent way with other believers in my class or at church. You never meant for me to be alone, not even now in medical school. As hard as it is for me, Lord, please grant me fellowship with believers that will keep my heart focused on you."

Questions to Ponder

1. Do you know any Christians in your medical school? Is there a Christian fellowship/church of which you are a part?

2. As a medical student, what challenges do you face in being part of a community of believers? Is there a part of you that resists being part of a Christian community? What does the author of Hebrews (see 3:12–13 and 10:24–25) say about this?

3. What does God say the church is (Ephesians 1:23), and what are we called to speak to and do for one another as the body of Christ (Eph. 4:29; 5:19)?

4. How can you encourage fellow believers today by reminding them why they are doing what they are doing?

5. How can you encourage someone today that studying God's creation is an opportunity to worship?

Chapter 8 Endnotes

1. Dietrich Bonhoeffer, *Life Together* (New York: HarperOne, 1954), 23.

2. *Instruments in the Redeemer's Hands*, 54.

3. Alan Medinger, *Journal of Biblical Counseling,* vol.13, no. 3 (Spring 1995): 54–55.

4. L. N. Dyrbye, M. R. Thomas, and J. L. Huntington, "Personal Life Events and Medical Student Burnout: A Multicenter Study," *Academic Medicine* (2006): 81:374–384.

   S. M. Willcock, M. G. Daly, C. C. Tennant, and B. J. Allard. "Burnout and Psychiatric Morbidity in New Medical Graduates," *Medical Journal of Australia* (2004): 181:357–360.

CHAPTER 9

Ministry Starts in Your First Year

What do you think of when you hear the word *ministering*? The *Merriam-Webster Dictionary* defines it as "to give aid or service." In the context of being a medical doctor, you may think of ministering as treating the socially disadvantaged or doing medical missions in developing countries. You may even have asked yourself at one time or another, "How can I serve people with my degree? How can I minister with my profession to those who are hurting?"

While ministering as a doctor of medicine is very much about serving those who are suffering, you must not forget that there is also an amazing opportunity for service and ministry from your very first day of medical school. Even before you face your first patient, your servant ministry can begin full-force with both believers and unbelievers studying around you. These four years of medical school (and more for those not from the Unites States or those in residency) are an opportunity to minister the gospel to your classmates and colleagues who will eventually be in a position to influence thousands, if not tens of thousands, in years to come. Seen in that light, what an incredible privilege it is that the Lord has placed you where you are!

A plastic surgery resident once told me that it was his conviction that the community of academic medicine was one of the world's unreached people groups. What better opportunity to share the love of Christ than among your fellow physicians-in-training while you study, learn, and toil together!

What exactly does "ministering" look like in medical school? Do you imagine an earnest and sincere believer, while sitting in class waiting for a lecture to start, turning to the person next to him and saying, "You know, God doesn't like medical students who don't appreciate him for his creation of the human body. You'd better believe in the Great Physician, because believe me, he's got some major surgery to do on you!" Or better yet, "Hey, aren't you glad we're studying cardiology? Your heart is so plagued with sin, you'll be needing a major transplant!" Obviously this is tongue-in-cheek, but if you think that sharing the gospel requires a confrontational, in-your-face stare-down with your classmate, at the end of the day you likely won't share the gospel at all.

Others prefer to retreat into the looming halls of medicine and blend conveniently into its shadows to avoid their calling as salt and light to the world. True ministering, however, is accomplished through openly sharing God's love. This is a calling that all Christians have been given. We are all priests of the new covenant. Not only have we all been given unique spiritual gifts to exercise, but we are called as God's children to exercise those gifts in love to those around us. (See 1 Corinthians 12; 1 John 4:11; Matthew 22:39). Mother Teresa once said, "We must know that we have been created for greater things, not just to be a number in the world, not just to go for diplomas and degrees, this work and that work. We have been created in order to love and to be loved. In order for us to be able to love, we need to have faith because faith is love in action; and love in action is service."[1] This is what it means to minister to our colleagues. It means to love them with God's love. Just how do we go about doing this?

Dr. Lloyd John Ogilvie gives us a good idea of what it means to share the love of God: "People are held in darkness until someone cares enough to share the Gospel with them in a way that they can see, understand, and accept the Truth. The world is desperate to know the love of God. But before they can know His love, they must first see His love in action. Jesus, the Light of the world, says to us, "You are the light of the world … Let your light shine before others, that they may see your good deeds and glorify your Father in heaven" (Matt. 5:14, 16).[2]

I kept much to myself during the first year of medical school, and sharing my faith did not come naturally. I rarely asked questions in class, and afterward I often went straight back to my apartment or to the library to study on my own. The times that I did spend with my classmates outside the classroom were in case-study groups or anatomy lab, which were to me an exercise in awkwardness. Part of the reason was that most of my college experience had been spent hanging around fellow believers, with only sparse interaction with nonbelievers. My Christian friends and I roomed, ate, played sports, studied, and took classes together. I was in as much of a holy huddle bubble as you could get.

Once medical school started, I found myself in the opposite situation. The majority of my "people time" was spent with non-Christians. It was hard to let go of my desire to stay safe with people who had values and desires similar to mine. God, however, had a much better plan. He provided opportunities in which I had to interact with classmates, and as a result, I got to know them better. In the process, I had to trust that he was with me every step of the way.

For example, during my first year, I took the simple step of eating dinner with my anatomy lab group. We began sharing stories and getting to know one another, and over time, we learned what made each of us laugh or smile, and even what things made us frustrated or angry. It took time, but the Lord caused me to truly care about who they were as people and not to avoid them, as had been my mentality in college. God is pleased when we take steps of faith in loving others. Mine were baby steps, but they were steps in the right direction.

There may be times, however, when you're invited to participate in activities you think may hinder your walk with God. For example, as much as medical students understand the harmful effects of certain vices—like consuming excessive alcohol or using drugs recreationally—they certainly are not immune to taking part in them. You may find yourself invited to join parties where such things are offered or even expected, with the understanding that it is time to let loose, especially after a round of exams. "Come on. You deserve it! It's time to drink up!" Instead of reflexively running in the opposite direction (or some may run toward it), be thoughtful about those opportunities to be with your classmates, and trust in the power of God and his wisdom to make the right choices.

This doesn't mean you should always participate in those activities. Instead, consider changing such an invitation into one of your own. You might say, "Sorry, I don't feel like going there, but how about meeting up for a good meal instead?" That way you aren't rejecting your classmates by not joining them. You are showing that you really are interested in spending time with them and that you can care for them without compromising your witness.

Other examples of loving them through Christ may include refraining from gossiping about classmates, speaking encouraging words to a fellow student who did not do well on an exam, or buying pizza for your late-night study group. Loving others with our deeds lets them see that the gospel has power to transform lives, beginning with our own. We show that we care because Christ cares, especially when the world is so consumed with itself and judging others.

"If Necessary, Use Words"

With that said, here is a brief reminder: loving others in action is not a substitute for sharing the gospel message. Both are vital, but it is in sharing the good news that we bring people from the kingdom of death and despair to the kingdom of life and hope. "But how can they call on Him if they have not put their trust in Him? And how can they put their trust in Him if they have not heard of Him? And how can they hear of Him unless someone tells them?" (Rom. 10:14 NLV).

The analogy of links on a chain may be helpful. Each link represents a believer, circumstance, or idea that a nonbeliever encounters, all of which lead up to the last link that the Lord uses to bring that soul to belief in Christ. You may be used by the Lord to prepare the heart of a person who is to be redeemed later on, or you may be the final link in the chain of God's work in that person's life. Regardless, be ready to ask the Lord for love and wisdom, as you prayerfully consider complementing your loving deeds with sharing the good news.

During the rigorous years of medical school, loving others seemed to me to be a Herculean task. However, these two reminders helped me—and can help you—possess a vision beyond the preoccupying busyness of school.

You can thrive, not just survive, in medical school.

Just as your physical muscles grow stronger when you exercise, so do your spiritual muscles as you exercise your faith. Don't give your spiritual life a break when life gets rough. Instead, see your circumstances as a spiritual exercise set in which your faith can and will be strengthened. Loving others can be hard; it can be tiresome; and there may be times when you think you just don't care anymore. Medical school certainly challenges your spiritual walk by crystallizing the truism, "No pain, no gain!" But don't throw in the towel. Take a step of faith, flex those muscles, and forge ahead in God's strength.

As you move forward, there is a second point to remember.

It is not about you. You can love others with the love of Christ, not your own.

If you have been a believer long enough, you know that going forth with gritted teeth, mustering up your courage, and striving in your own strength ("I just *have* to love you") will lead to burnout. Your fire for serving the Lord will quickly cool, and what remains can be the ashes of your faith.

Instead, acknowledge that loving in a manner worthy of the Lord cannot be accomplished through your selfish nature. It comes only by dependently walking with him in faith. That is why Jesus said, "My grace is sufficient for you, for my power is made perfect in weakness." Paul walked in this truth and rejoiced: "Therefore I will boast all the more gladly about my weaknesses, so that Christ's power may rest on me. That is why, for Christ's sake, I delight in weaknesses, in insults, in hardships, in persecutions, in difficulties. For when I am weak, then I am strong" (2 Cor. 12:9–10).

Confess to the Lord your inability to love others wholly and consistently in your own strength, and instead trust in the unquenchable, all-wise, and perfect love of Christ to work through you. He promises to provide for you a supernatural power and ability to care for and love your peers in a way that you could not do on your own. Thank God for that, and then move forward by his strength and in his love!

Suggested Prayer

"Father, when it comes to ministering to my classmates, I confess that I come up with so many excuses. I make sharing the gospel a lot harder than it should be. Sometimes I just don't want to rock the boat. Sometimes I worry what people think of me. Sometimes I just don't feel like it. Break all the misconceptions in my soul that keep me from sharing your good news. Let the fullness of the gospel message flow out of me as I do what you've called me to do with my classmates and those around me: to love them as you have loved me. Give me your heart to love them. Let them see Christ in me, that the gospel would be made known to them in word and deed. Open doors of opportunity to love them. Let me be sensitive to your Spirit's leading, and give me the wisdom to obey. Be glorified in all I do and say."

Questions to Ponder

1. What thoughts have you had about serving God with your medical degree? Have you thought about how you, as a medical student, could serve God at this very moment?
2. When you minister to your classmates, you love them. How can you love your classmates even today?
3. What experiences in medical school have challenged you to compromise God's standards? How can you respond in a way that shows you care for the people around you but that also keeps you from discrediting your witness?
4. Is there someone you can think of whom you can love in action as well as with the gospel message? Pray that the Spirit would open doors for you and give you his courage and his love to be a minister of the gospel to that person.

Chapter 9 Endnotes

1. Mother Teresa, *No Greater Love* (New York: New World Library, 1997) 29–30, 32.
2. *Helping the World to See*, compiled by Lor Cunningham (Bensheim, Germany: Christian Blind Mission International, Inc., 1988), 21.

CHAPTER 10

Relationships in Medical School: Destination or Distraction?

As a single twenty-something in medical school, I craved companionship. Even though I felt as if I had no time for a relationship, I still wanted one. After graduating from college, my friends had left for the working world, even as I transitioned into the daunting world of medical training. And with the ensuing lack of fellowship, I struggled with what I thought were competing desires of wanting a significant other and being academically successful. Would I even have time to build or establish a relationship? I didn't think my time constraints would be fair to any potential girlfriend—or to my studies. With limited time in the day, these desires appeared to be mutually exclusive.

Enter God. In my second year of school, God opened my eyes to the woman who would eventually become my wife. At the time, she was a young undergraduate, so despite my growing interest in her, I was convicted that I needed to give her time to grow in her own right before she became attached to anyone else. She was still growing and finding herself, and I wanted to be sure that she had the freedom and opportunity to do that through God's leading, not mine. In college I had seen young couples become exclusive to the point where they no longer developed or matured in their relationships with their church community, family, or friends. When those relationships ended (and who expects that they ever will?), they were left with no one they could turn to, because they had left their respective friends months and even years earlier.

My future wife didn't share my philosophy, however, so she happily dated several people over the next couple of years—very much to my chagrin! But as the Lord would have it, she and I eventually began dating three years after we first met (and even then I was concerned I was rushing into things). Yet despite our vastly different philosophies on dating, God worked gloriously and graciously in both of us, and three years after that, we were married. Balancing our relationship in medical school and residency was not easy, but I discovered that it certainly was not impossible. Despite its challenges, the covenant of marriage is sweet, and the spiritual fruits we are even now experiencing are refining us more and more into Christlikeness.

When I was single, I often wondered how I could possibly meet someone, given my busy schedule. Would my only recourse be to marry another doctor or health-care worker and hold out hope that she was not too busy for me? If you have no deep, platonic relationships in medical school, as was my case, your desire for a romantic relationship can be very intense. How you respond to this desire is crucially important in your walk with the Lord.

Some people settle for compromises. For example, you might be tempted to enter a relationship with someone who doesn't share your faith but whom you see frequently in class or at the hospital. Such relationships typically become ones of convenience rather than ones through which God is glorified. Some people seek respite from their desire for a relationship through pornography. Others fall into depression—depending on where they are geographically, life can be very difficult during the long, cold winter months. It can seem as if no one really cares about, or can identify with, your struggles.

If you do have a spouse or significant other in medical school, not all your problems are solved, as you well know. Medical school and time spent at the hospital can bring a new and stressful dynamic to your relationship. Because of your schedule, there may be days when you do not see your spouse at all. If your spouse is not in the health-care field, you may wonder whether he or she really understands what you're going through, and that seeming disconnect can be a point of contention. You might feel even more isolated or misunderstood by your significant other as you learn to juggle your relationship with one hand and school with the other—both of which demand all your energy and attention at the same time.

Whether you are single or married, you might find yourself asking, as I did: "Is this all there is? Where is God in all of this frustration, confusion, loneliness, and deep desire?"

True Satisfaction

We have to constantly remind ourselves that only in a relationship with the living Christ can we find real wholeness and contentedness. For a season, a significant other can and often does bring a sense of fulfillment, but inevitably it cannot satisfy the deepest longing of our hearts. It is unfair to ask a fallible human being to meet a supernatural relational need that only God can fill. Only God can keep that promise to be our source of true fulfillment, whatever our relationship status in life. Our spouse or significant other can certainly provide a measure of love, security, and encouragement, but even those emotions originate from the deep wellspring of God's love.

God's love for us is not an abstract concept, as much as we might think it is. How do we know that God really has a deep and abiding love for us? He did not notice a sliver of goodness in you or me, and think, "Well, he seems like an okay person. I suppose I'll love him." No, he loved us when there was nothing good in us at all. It was from within his very nature that he chose to love. "For a good person someone might possibly dare to die. But God demonstrates his own love for us in this: While we were still sinners, Christ died for us" (Rom. 5:7–8).

There was no righteousness in us when Christ took our sins upon the cross. And yet Jesus died and rose again for us. This was no halfhearted effort! What more proof of his love could we ask for? What more do we need? Let us be thankful that our Creator knows our deepest hungers, longings, and desires, and yet he still chose to die for us. Before we go looking for human relationships, let us worship and praise him for giving us the greatest relationship we could ever have.

An Action Plan

Relationships are a tremendous blessing, but if God chooses not to give you one in medical school, instead of dwelling in bitterness or self-pity ("I'm not good enough" or "I'm going to be a spinster because life stinks"), consider praising God instead. How so? Let him have your heart—your feelings of despair, anger, sadness, or confusion—as you bow before him in worship. Remember, you shouldn't stop worshipping God just because you don't feel like it. It is not disingenuous to pray or sing to him when you don't feel like it. In fact, we're commanded to worship, regardless of how we feel, simply because he is worthy.

God knows exactly what he is doing in your life, and his plan is perfect. This doesn't mean you need to conjure up "happy feelings" in your prayers, as if he didn't already know how you really felt. As you pray, you can ask him earnestly to bring you a joyful faith.

When I have stumbled into church after a tiring night on call or a particularly difficult exam, I've prayed this prayer many times: "Father, right now I don't feel like worshipping you, but I know you command me to do so. I confess my lack of desire. Please give me the desire to worship you as I sing and read and listen to your Word." Even this little act of faith was heard by the Lord, and almost every time he graciously granted me an uplifted and restored heart. Even when he didn't, I still worshipped the worthy King.

God sees our worship as an exercise of faith, and it brings him pleasure. God will take us from where we are, even in the midst of our weak faith, and bring us closer to him. An example of this is found in Mark 9:21–27, where a father pleaded with Jesus to help his son, who was possessed by an evil spirit. The father admitted his own weak and faltering faith and asked Jesus to help him with his unbelief. Jesus did not retort angrily, "You must have perfect faith for me to listen to you or to save your son!" Instead he took the father's faith where it was, and in his loving power, he performed a miracle in the possessed child. Because the father actively sought Jesus in and through his struggling faith ("I believe; help my unbelief!"), the Lord honored his request and blessed him through it.

Dating Guidelines

Should singles actively pursue dating in medical school? There is, I think, no uniform answer to that question. A relationship could very well be central to God's plans for you during those years, although it is often hard to tell just by cognitively analyzing your circumstances. God often works in surprising ways. Thus it is critical to keep your motives in check. Beware of falling into the habit of "shopping" for the ideal person. This can lead to a market mentality. People are not products. They are not to be approached as if they exist only for your consumption. Resist the temptation to look at another person as you ask yourself, "Does this person fit my criteria for meeting my needs?" We too often forget the more important question: "How can I serve this person and bring this person into a deeper love of Christ?"

Being others-centered is a prerequisite for entering any kind of personal relationship. Are you living each day looking to satisfy your selfish cravings and sin-centered desires? Or are you living life for God by seeking ways to serve others? For example, do you choose to dress provocatively in order to draw the attention of others in a sensual way? Do you allow your mind to wander toward lustful imaginations, as you linger over racy internet or television ads? Are you coveting or judging others' relationships ("Oh, he's such a good catch—he's w-a-a-a-y too good for her")? These are all examples of how a healthy longing for relationship can be hijacked by the sinful nature, giving in to what the world calls "your every right to do and say whatever you want, because that is just the way things work." Instead of giving in, why not take on the challenge that Christ gives his people by taking every thought captive for Christ and being a servant to all (2 Cor. 10:5)?

Whatever your conviction regarding dating in medical school, strive to be faithful to what God has called you to do at this very moment. In his providential timing, I eventually met my wife-to-be, when, despite the temptation to skip out on church, I chose to attend worship consistently. You may or may not meet your future spouse in a similar manner, but it is important to be faithful now in what you are called to do and be. Do your work well and study diligently unto the Lord. Don't give up meeting with the fellowship of believers. Actively pursue—and be—the kind of person you value and seek.

Couples Guidelines

For those already married, you know the strain that can result from the time and energy needed for your studies and hospital work. Less time together and more work can tax even the strongest relationships. The same principles apply: seek Christ first. Seek him by praying with and for each other. Make deliberate efforts to share God's truth with each other, including putting your spouse's needs above your own. As you rely wholeheartedly on God, let him open your eyes to see his power working in you as you trust him with your marriage and your studies.

Whether you are single or married, there are several books that are highly recommended reading. You may not agree with everything written in them, and that is okay, but let these books open your mind to ways of approaching relationships other than our society's "what can I get out of this" mentality. These include: *The Mystery of Marriage: Meditations on the Miracle* by Mike Mason, *Crazy Love: Overwhelmed by a Relentless God* by Francis Chan, *I Kissed Dating Goodbye* and *Boy Meets Girl* by Joshua Harris, *Boundaries in Dating: Making Dating Work* by Henry Cloud and John Townsend, *Love and Respect* by Emerson Eggerich, and *The Five Love Languages: The Secret to Love that Lasts* by Gary Chapman. The Christian Medical and Dental Associations (CMDA) also has wonderful weekend retreats that take place around the country, encouraging and teaching couples how to navigate the challenges of being in a medical marriage.

Suggested Prayer

"Lord, this is a lesson I know I need to learn: that regardless of the state I am in (single or in a relationship), my relationship with you, Lord, is the greatest one that I can ever have. You left the comforts of heaven and took on the form of a human being to die on the cross for my sins. This is a sacrifice that I am just beginning to comprehend. I pray that even when I don't feel like worshipping you, I would acknowledge that feeling to you and worship you anyway, for you are worthy. Change those feelings as I seek you first, Jesus, before all other relationships. Transform me, so that instead of looking for ways to fulfill my own desires and interests, I would look to serve and love others, just as you serve and love me even today. Be my hope, my joy, my peace, my satisfaction, and my all."

Questions to Ponder

1. How do you feel about starting or maintaining a relationship while in medical school? Are there any challenges you face right now concerning that?
2. Why is it important to first understand our depravity in order to comprehend the love of God for us?
3. How is Christ's love able to truly fulfill you, regardless of your relationship status?
4. The next time you find yourself struggling in the area of relationships, how can you worship God in the midst of your struggle, especially if you don't feel like it?
5. If you do pursue a relationship in school (or are already in one), what can you do to be more others- and Christ-centered with that person?

CHAPTER 11

"God's Scientific Method" by Richard Chung

In your schooling, you'll likely be exposed to the workings of research across a variety of related disciplines. Within medical academia, new knowledge is treasured, productivity and publishing is revered, and always-too-sparse funding is coveted. At first blush, research seemed to me a bit like the Tower of Babel, with humans grasping for godly knowledge of the details of the human body in the midst of disease. Academicians ask questions, state hypotheses, and then go about testing their hypotheses in stiff and sterile environments, while real people suffer in the streets of our communities, and accolades resulting from any research accomplishments are bestowed without acknowledgment of the one who created the very things they research.

However, through a combination of patient care (yielding a deeper appreciation of the bounty that came from research) as well as my own experience, I slowly began to view research from a broader perspective and to see how God uses it for his eternal purposes. I realized that my initial impressions were naïve, that they underestimated God's presence and work in science. As with innumerable other things in life, God can use human and even seemingly secular pursuits to further his kingdom purposes. Research is no different. It is enormously God-glorifying to unveil the secrets of God's universe.

Rigorous scientific research is not a threat to God. Instead, it is a rich means of revealing more of his glory to the eyes of those who don't know him. Antony Flew, a philosopher and former atheist, once said, "It now seems to me that the findings of more than fifty years of DNA research have provided materials for a new and enormously powerful argument to design."[1]

The more we learn about the world, the more evidence we accrue that the world was intricately designed by God. Romans 1:19–20 (ESV) states, "For what can be known about God is plain to them, because God has shown it to them. For his invisible attributes, namely, his eternal power and divine nature, have been clearly perceived, ever since the creation of the world, in the things that have been made. So they are without excuse." God reveals his wonder and glory, and whether that fundamental realization brings one to a saving knowledge of Christ is up to God's plan.

Although medical research is, at its core, about the acquisition of new knowledge, it is the acquisition of knowledge with the purpose of relieving suffering and healing the bits and pieces of the brokenness of this world. Research is founded in and motivated by the experiences and suffering of people. As such, medical research is a means of justice, with the hope of righting the wrongs that sickness has bestowed. This aspect of research screams of the redemptive purposes of God and his overall plan, which will culminate in his future return.

As I began thinking about it more, I realized that God created research. He gave us this activity as a means of revealing more and more of the wonder of his creation. Paul Davies, an astrophysicist, comments, "There is for me powerful evidence that there is something going on behind it all ... It seems as though somebody has fine-tuned nature's numbers to make the Universe ... The impression of design is overwhelming."[2] Instead of deconstructing God's creation and bringing it closer to man, research reveals the depths and complexities of creation, making it bigger and more glorious to behold. Man is not building or creating anything through research. He is simply unpacking and understanding more of God's immaculate and intricate creation.

Certainly, some researchers may approach their efforts with self-aggrandizing motivations, as the apparent discovery of new knowledge is undeniably intoxicating. However, even in doing so, they unwittingly serve God's purposes in further revealing his creation. If you feel led to a research career, do not shy away on account of similar misconceptions. Instead, know that everything in creation is God's, even research labs. The next time you are in a lab or working on a research project, dare to breathe a prayer of thanksgiving to the God who gave us the wondrous privilege of discovering his brilliant mind through his intricate creation, as well as partaking in the process of learning how to heal and redeem sickness and disease.

Whether we see it clearly or not, God is working everywhere. Christians need to venture wholeheartedly into places that suffer from a dearth of God's people, and medical academia is certainly one of those places. As always, stay focused and keep your eyes on God, but run toward the calling of research, if God has laid that path before you.

Suggested Prayer

"Lord, your universe is a vast world of yet-undiscovered truth. We are just beginning to uncover it, and that can be very exciting. I pray that I would be able to see your hand at work, even in the discovery of new knowledge, and that I would use it as an opportunity to worship you. If you give me the opportunity for research, give me a clear, logical, and creative mind in my discovery of truth, a pure heart in being honest and ethical with my data, and a spirit of humility, as I acknowledge that you are the Lord of creation. Reveal your handiwork as I seek you. Let the work I do, even today, bring honor to you."

Questions to Ponder

1. How have you seen scientific research reveal the complexity and beauty of God's creation?
2. How does the creation or discovery of new knowledge reveal aspects of God's personal and creative spirit?
3. How do you create an attitude of worshipping God when it comes to research?

Chapter 11 Endnotes

1. "Atheist Becomes Theist: Exclusive Interview with Former Atheist Anthony Flew," *Philosophia Christos*, Vol. 6, No. 2 (Winter 2004).
2. Paul Davies, *The Cosmic Blueprint: New Discoveries in Nature's Creative Ability to Order the Universe* (New York: Simon and Schuster, 1988), 203.

CHAPTER 12

In the Classroom and among Your Peers: An Attitude Adjustment

By my second year of medical school, I had gotten a feel for what my classmates were like. There were the inordinately bright ones who always did well on exams, the class clowns who interjected lightness into an often heavy atmosphere, and the others who, for whatever reason, seemed to get on everyone's nerves.

There was always a nagging sense of uncertainty about how, in the midst of an academically competitive environment, I was to interact with all of these different personalities in a God-honoring way. I was challenged to be salt and light to those around me, while at the same time struggling to stay afloat in my studies. There was also the self-inflicted conflict of feeling judged by others, based on how quickly I responded to questions in class or in my case-study group. Whenever answers evaded me, while my peers piped up quickly, my feelings of inadequacy mingled with those of jealousy and reluctant humility. Was I supposed to ignore the inward discord and instead think, *Everything's gonna be all right. Let's just praise the Lord*? That felt disingenuous and did not reflect what I was truly feeling. Fortunately, the Bible has something to say about this.

The Superficial Moralist

One dangerous perspective that Christian medical students can bring into the classroom is the moralistic, superficial, "I'm doing absolutely super-fantastic, thank you very much!" To people who hold this view, anything less effusive is frowned upon as unspiritual or even sinful. The implication is that "real Christians" don't struggle. This, however, is empty spiritual fluff, because it ignores God's ability to deeply encourage us in the midst of real trials and truly difficult struggles.

The moralistic approach to relating to peers is achieved by minimizing your interactions with them as much as possible and putting on a mask that indicates that "everything is just fine," when actually it is not. Whether or not you chalk it up to a superficial Christian subculture (such as growing up in a family riddled with hostility and strife that put on a mask and acted perfectly harmonious at church), the idea that Christians are supposed to always be happy is unbiblical and unhealthy for your spiritual walk.

In the Psalms, we find that King David frequently groaned before God as he was chased by his own son, fell prostrate in agony before God, and was plagued by guilt stemming from his adulterous affair with Bathsheba. Discouragement and bouts of angst colored David's life, and he acknowledged it before the one who saw the good and bad of it all. Jesus, too, displayed the whole gamut of emotion, from righteous anger to tears (Matt. 21:12–13; John 11:33–36), yet he was without sin (Heb. 4:15). God's chosen people brought their real and honest emotions before him. We shouldn't grieve God by pretending we're feeling something we're not. He already knows!

The Worldly Humanist

An opposite and equally dangerous perspective is the go-with-the-flow approach, in which circumstances become king and your academic performance determines how you feel. There were times when I felt that I was acting as if my faith had no bearing on my life in medical school, something I now refer to as being "a duped believer." This is someone who believes that his walk with God has nothing to do with his interactions with his classmates. His main concern is looking good in front of them. Desiring respect, he never admits weakness or shares the struggles he may have. His spiritual life is a roller coaster, because his sense of well-being hinges on the next test, the next evaluation, or the next board exam. He has become so comfortable among his nonbelieving peers that there is essentially nothing that distinguishes him from the rest of his class.

John, one of my classmates, shared such concerns with me. He lamented how hypocritical he felt, because his actions around his classmates did not reflect his identity in Christ. "It originally started as fear of offending those I wanted to witness to," he said, "but now I think I have just become too comfortable with being worldly." He had started out attempting to show grace to his nonbelieving classmates, but in the end, he slipped into self-interested comfort. He was not dealing with an attitude problem but a heart problem. The desire of his heart had been misplaced away from God and into pleasing himself and others. When he began insisting on doing things his way to the neglect of God's desires for him, he became—simply put—prideful.

Beyond causing us to puff ourselves up when we do well, pride also causes shame and embarrassment when we fail. Put another way, our desire for the affection of our peers is not just about that adulation itself but also about avoiding the opposite: not appearing good enough for them. This is particularly true in medical school, which takes habitually successful students and places them in the midst of often equally or more successful peers. Such a change can be a shock to the system for someone who has grown accustomed to being a step ahead of others.

I found myself in that situation and often berated myself when things didn't go the way I'd planned. Why were my classmates able to spout the material more thoroughly than I could? Why didn't the usual amount of time I had spent studying achieve for me the same results as it had in college? I was trying hard to reclaim my sense of self through achievements, better grades, and publishing papers. When taken in their proper context, these are all worthy goals in themselves, but for me they became cravings I had to satisfy at almost any cost. Over time, and with the gracious patience of God, I began to see the worldly perspective I was taking on and the devious nature of pride.

Oddly enough, it was a sixteenth-century monk, John of Landsberg, who seemed to understand my plight as a Christian student, struggling (and sometimes failing) to validate myself with accomplishments:

> One thing I have to warn you of especially is your constant tendency to grow fainthearted under the weight of your faults and oversights and an inclination almost to despair when a sudden lack of confidence reduces your firm decisions to nothing. I know those moods when you sit there utterly alone, eaten up with unhappiness, in a pure state of grief. You don't move towards me but desperately imagine that everything you have ever done has been utterly lost and forgotten. This near-despair and self-pity are actually a form of pride. What you think was a state of absolute security from which you've fallen was really trusting too much in your own strength and

ability. Profound depression and perplexity of mind often follow a loss of hope, when what really ails you is that things simply haven't happened as you expected and wanted. In fact, I don't want you to rely on your own strength and abilities and plans, but to distrust them and to distrust yourself, and to trust me and no one and nothing else. As long as you rely on yourself you are bound to come to grief. You still have a most important lesson to learn: Your own strength will no more help you to stand upright than dropping yourself on a broken reed. You must not despair of me. You must hope and trust in me absolutely. My mercy is infinite.[1]

The Gospel Perspective

There is a third perspective. It is the gospel-centered perspective. Despite the fact that discouragement and despair can invade one's life, hope ultimately rules the day. In dealing with the competitive nature of the classroom, understanding and acknowledging your struggle before God is the first step to achieving a God-centered view. We are not holy ghosts who float above the struggles of sinful people. We are eminently prone to feelings of jealousy, unrighteous anger, prideful condescension, and many other ungodly attitudes. That comes with being human. However, we have been given the resources and power in Christ to overcome these sinful tendencies and instead see our peers as those whom God has called us to love sacrificially.

This is where the rule of Christ can encourage us. We are on a journey of life (not just medical school) to become more like him. When God brought us from death to life, our reason for living became to give him glory. We need to understand that life is more than fulfilling our desires and dreams. It centers on fulfilling *his* glory and *his* desires. God put you in medical school to expand his kingdom, not yours. When it feels as if your very self is being attacked or threatened by another's abilities or accomplishments, rest in this truth: your value is not based on your cognitive capacity, the breadth of your medical insight, or what others think of you. It is based on the blood that brought sinners like you and me into a living relationship with a righteous and holy God. Nothing can change that, and its surety should be your unshakable foundation of hope and purpose in this life.

Jesus himself knew the purpose of his time on earth, and his acts of humble service did not diminish his kingship, sovereignty, or power. His identity was not threatened by washing his disciples' feet. Likewise, you need not be intimidated by your peers as you seek to serve them. You can truly enjoy them for who they are without placing upon them the unnecessary burden and unachievable goal of being the reason for your joy and worth. Instead, God is glorified when, by his supernatural Spirit, you exercise the power he gives you to love others!

Is there something wrong with desiring the respect of my peers, celebrating accomplishments, and hoping for a top residency position? No. But when something good takes the place of something great—when something that is wanted becomes the must-have thing that rules my heart (and therefore my actions), I become idolatrous. Overcome this spirit of compromise by relying daily on the presence of Christ and reminding yourself of his continuing work in you. Come to him in humble repentance, and also in the hope and assurance that his mercies are new every day, knowing that he can renew your motivations, desires, and hopes to be in line with his.

Suggested Prayer

"God, I confess that many times, instead of knowing and living the Christian life as you've called me to, I've chosen to live in a way that is most convenient to me. At the root of this is pride. Forgive me, Lord, for making everything all about me. Make me like David, a person who longed after your heart and who acknowledged and repented of his sins before you. You know how I feel, and I don't need to hide my feelings from you. I bring before you my feelings of insecurity, my being unreal in order to protect myself, and the compromises I've made in order to fit in with my classmates. Lord, I repent of these attitudes and pray for a deep, kingdom-glorifying, and Christ-centered heart. I bring my struggles and feelings before you and pray that you would continue to do your work in me, changing me and making me more and more like Christ."

Questions to Ponder

1. Have you ever struggled with feeling inferior or even incompetent compared to your peers? Do you think this affects the way you interact with them?
2. Have you ever felt the pressure to pretend that for you, as a Christian, everything is going "super-fantastically well"? What does the Bible say about this, and what examples are there of people who acknowledged their suffering and trials and yet were considered by God to be godly?
3. On the flip side, have you lived in a way in which your circumstances dictated whether you chose to follow God? What does this usually say about the desires of our hearts?
4. What do you think about the comment: "Beyond causing us to brag or puff ourselves up when we do well, pride also causes shame and embarrassment when we fail"?

5. What is the gospel's perspective, when it comes to working in a competitive environment? What can you do today to be reminded of your true, unshakable value in Christ?

Chapter 12 Endnotes

1. John of Landsberg (1555), "On Pride: A Letter from Jesus Christ to the Soul that Really Loves Him," *The Gospel Transformation Workbook 2002* (Jenkintown, Penn.: World Harvest Mission, 2002), 56.

CHAPTER 13

A Human Pathology: How to Glorify God When Everything Goes Wrong

In the thick of my second-year studies, I was faced with the troubling question: how can one glorify God in studying human pathology? In contrast to my first year, when studying the intricacies of the human body pointed to the greatness of God's design and ingenuity, the material I now had to learn seemed to have none of the promptings toward thanksgiving or praise. Giving thanks for something like diabetes, cancer, or genetic malformations seemed like a terribly twisted thing to do.

The amount of data to be learned was also several orders of magnitude greater than in my first year. There is only one heart, one set of lungs, and one central nervous system, but there is a multitude of disease processes that affect them. I had to bear the frustrating and painful process of intense memorization, countless hours of study in the library, and cramming for Step 1 of the boards that were coming that summer. It was panning out to be an academically difficult year.

My second year brought other challenges as well. The terrorist attacks of September 11, 2001, occurred that year and served to make painfully obvious where I was placing my hopes at the time.

Essentially, my hope was in providing a secure and safe lifestyle, perhaps finding a high-paying job in a popular city and living in wealthy suburbia.

Furthermore, the never-ending stress of four exams every three weeks was taking its grinding toll, and my mental, physical, and spiritual life began spiraling downward. Exercise and building friendships were at the bottom of my priority list. Whenever I was with my classmates, I saw them as competitors and potential backstabbers rather than friends and colleagues. Instead of trusting them, I decided to protect myself from their potential ridicule or competition and save face by proudly hiding my struggles. I preferred isolation and plowing through the work on my own. Although my time in the Word was consistent, the quality and richness of it, as well as my depth of worship in church, were not.

Thus began the insidious, downward pull. There was no single event or situation during my second year that precipitated my spiritual descent. It was the gradual hammering away of my inner reserves and giving in to the temptation to look out for my own interests. Reflecting on the growing pathology I saw in my own life— ironically, while studying medical pathology at the same time—I gradually began to develop a better perspective on dealing with the brokenness that exists, not only in the human body but also in ourselves.

Sin's Disease

After Adam sinned, his descendants and the world, thereafter, became entombed in moral, spiritual, and physical death. Our bodies, though incredibly designed, malfunction and are susceptible to the environment's unrelenting attacks. What we see in textbooks and eventually the wards is a visible manifestation of the fallenness and mortality of the human race. Physical illness isn't an analogy of sin. It *is* sin's reality.

For example, because of my sinfulness, I sleep too little. My pride and worry keep me awake, which takes a toll on my health. Similarly, illnesses and suffering may lead me into bitterness and rejection of God. Despite our human instinct to avoid suffering, and because of our sinfulness, we often contribute to that suffering through our decisions, whether purposely or unwittingly. And though there are direct, causal relationships between sinful acts and illness, in many cases, this is not so. Take, for example, the patient who receives a lifesaving blood transfusion but acquires HIV in the process. Whatever the means, sin has its way of affecting all of humanity. So how can you, as a medical student, battle such a pervasive enemy?

Know Your Enemy

A cipher device known as the "Enigma machine" was used by the Nazis in World War II to transmit encoded messages to its military. This machine consisted of a complex set of electrical and mechanical systems that encoded messages based on the machine's configuration. As long as the recipient had the key, he could easily decipher the code. Without it, the potential key options ran into the trillions.

The Nazi military knew that the Enigma was not perfect, but they refused to believe that the Allies would undertake the massive effort required to decode it. The Nazis were wrong. Over the course of the war, Allied mathematicians and military intelligence—with the aid of captured hardware and key tables—broke the code and intercepted several hundred thousand messages. Through understanding their enemy's tactics and movements, Allied forces were able to defeat a powerful foe.

In a similar manner, your grasp of disease processes will better equip you to effectively battle the wages of sin, including human frailty and its susceptibility to sickness. When you pore over the multitude of diseases that barrage the body, remind yourself that these things are a very real reflection of humankind's brokenness. "So you want me to think about the misfortunes and disease of sin for an entire year?" you might ask. Why not? You are at war with an enemy called *disease*.

When you study how each organ system falls to illness, you are gathering intelligence on the enemy's strategies. You first learned how the body functions as a system, how each organ works, and how tissues and cells repair and heal normally. Now you are growing in the knowledge of how disease and brokenness affect it. When you study how genetic anomalies, bacterial invasions, and cancerous cells relentlessly attack the body, your knowledge will grow as you learn of the relationship between the body's healing mechanisms and its brokenness. To put it another way: knowing the enemy's strategy is the first step toward defeating it.

Being Redeemer-Oriented

One of the amazing truths about the Christian life is that death and illness are not how God intends things to ultimately end. Dwelling on the seriousness and utter ugliness of sin's effects makes the beauty of God's redeeming mission for his people that much more magnificent. Jewelers display their diamonds on entirely black backgrounds so that the stones' radiance and splendor can be more fully appreciated. Likewise, when we see how sick humankind can become, we can turn thoughts of hopelessness into worship, as we thank God for the opportunity to bring true hope to a very dark world.

The fact that we are required to learn so much about what goes wrong should challenge us to remember that a great day is coming when there will be no more pain, suffering, or death, and that God is using us to usher in his kingdom, here and now. As physicians-in-training who are living between the time of Jesus' resurrection and his second coming, we have the unique privilege of engaging in the redemptive act of healing as heralds of this coming and glorious day. Our involvement as agents of redemption is not just an analogy of God's future plan for mankind but of a present-day reality. We are instruments and tools of God, bringing people to wholeness—the way they are supposed to be.

Suggested Prayer

"Lord, I know that sin's effect on the world is very real. It is so entrenched in us that, apart from you, I know there is no hope. I pray that you would bring me more awareness of my sin, not for the purpose of condemnation but as an invitation to partake in your continuing redemptive work in my life. You desire that I not be driven by guilt but by hope. Forgive me of my sins, Lord. I also pray that in my studies you would help sharpen and enlarge my mind to learn the multitude of pathologies that affect the body so that ultimately I might be better able to heal them. Give me wisdom in my studies. As I learn how damaging sin's effects are, turn my heart to worship, even as I look to the Redeemer who one day will make all things whole again. I want to be used by you to bring hope into this world. Make me a blessing to those around me today."

Questions to Ponder

1. Although you may not have a physical disease, how does understanding the true state of your spiritual pathology (for example, Jeremiah 17:9 says, "The heart is deceitful above all

things") help you give thanks to your healer and redeemer, Jesus Christ?

2. How can the analogy of a diamond on a black background reflect how you can worship God through the pathology you study?

3. Give thanks to God this day for providing you with the opportunity to be engaged in his redemptive process—from the ugliness of sin's effects to healing and wholeness.

CHAPTER 14

The Clinical Interview: Bringing Light to the Conversation

It's not difficult to ask a question like, "What brings you to the hospital today?" It's asking the more personal questions that drives home the fact that you have opened a privileged door to the intimate details of a patient's life. When I first began interviewing, it seemed as if it took forever to get past the awkwardness of asking about someone's illicit drug use, their number of sexual partners, or even the date of their last menstrual cycle. These are certainly not topics to broach with acquaintances over tea and crackers! However, your journey from embarrassment to proficiency in the clinical setting is not only an important skill to learn, but a God-provided opportunity to minister his acceptance and love to another.

During my medical interviewing course, one of the first patients I met had just been admitted to the cardiac ward. After breathing a quick prayer, I knocked on the door and entered to see an elderly man, sitting on the side of the bed, his back facing me as he stared out the window of the tenth floor, apparently lost in thought. I coughed and introduced myself, asking if I could ask him some questions. He agreed, so I started off with what I thought was an easy question: "So, what brings you to the hospital today?" Slowly he turned toward me, his face ashen, and in a shaking, quiet voice, he muttered, "The doctor told me I need heart bypass surgery." Apparently, the surgeon had delivered the news just moments before I arrived. Numb from the unexpected news, the man had been left alone to decide if he wanted to go through with it.

I considered my own options at that moment. Should I back out apologetically and leave? Should I ask if he needed a minister? Right then, however, I felt as if I received a gentle nudge from God that he had placed me there at that moment simply to listen. Despite my sorely lacking clinical skills, this man needed someone to talk to. The class requirement was only to ask him a handful of questions regarding his stay at the hospital, but I was able to spend more time, asking not only about his illness but also about his life. He shared about his family that he missed, his sadness about the situation, and his fears about the sudden need for surgery. He also shared simply how thankful he was that I was spending time with him.

At the end of our conversation, I offered gently to pray with him, and he gladly agreed. It was an opportunity to minister to him in his moment of despair—and a blessing for me to see God work in bringing him comfort.

The Confidence of Christ

It is only natural that we might begin our medical training feeling uncertain about our abilities to assess a patient. When I first started out, I always wondered if one of my patients would glare at me impatiently and growl, "Okay, son, now how about a real doctor?" I worried that if they really knew how uncertain I was in my interviewing or physical exam skills, I would lose their trust. It was tempting to stretch my knowledge and lie between my teeth, pretending to know all the answers. How else could I gain the patient's trust? What if, after I auscultated a patient's apparently normal heart, he asked me how his murmur sounded? What would I say then?

The first important truth to know is that being confident in your interactions with others is not the same as knowing all the answers. Your confidence before others is based on Christ's steadfast love for you. Because of his love, not knowing an answer does not need to paralyze you in embarrassment or shame. It is a confidence based outside of yourself that cannot be hindered by what you know or don't know. There is freedom in saying, "I don't know, but I'll find out the answer." Being honest motivates you to fill in the gaps of your knowledge base because someone else can hold you accountable. You can breathe a sigh of relief, because in Christ you have been given the power to be free from the prison of trying to impress those around you for the sake of saving face or establishing your self-worth.

A Calling to Keep Our Patients' Confidence

"What you heard from me, keep as the pattern of sound teaching, with faith and love in Christ Jesus. Guard the good deposit that was entrusted to you—guard it with the help of the Holy Spirit who lives in us" (2 Tim. 1:13–14).

In this passage, Paul was referring to believers who had been entrusted with the gospel of truth and were commanded to guard this precious gift. The gospel has been given to us to be taken seriously, allowing it to transform our heart's desires and empower Christ's living through us. When our patients see that we truly value them as individuals and protect what they say in confidence, we "guard" the teaching of Christ: that he loves his people and sees them not as a means to an end, but as his precious, dearly loved children. In other words, we can care for and protect the patient's personal information with the goal of moving them toward healing, because God created each and every person as eternally valuable and important. Through your love and commitment to Christ, you are not just practicing good medicine; you are reflecting a gospel-focused heart by bringing God's kingdom of love to the patients you are taking care of.

Addressing the Spiritual Aspects of Health

But what about a patient's spiritual needs? Is that part of medicine too? Yes! A growing body of research has shown that the spiritual well-being of a patient is significantly tied to his or her health. The Joint Commission has made the point that patients' spirituality should be respected, acknowledged, and addressed as part of their medical care.[1] A commentary in 2008 from the Journal of the American Medical Association (JAMA) also noted the importance of an integrative approach to care, stating that "forging a spiritual connection among … any patient and his or her significant others—can restore a sense of control, meaning, and the ability to cope."[2] This is in line with what the majority of patients already believe, which is that a doctor should be aware of and talk to them about their spiritual beliefs. Unfortunately, the doctor's discomfort with these topics is a significant barrier to addressing them.

Is it possible to ethically and professionally incorporate the patient's spiritual beliefs and sources of hope into his or her diagnosis, prognosis, and treatment? Absolutely. In fact, as a Christian medical student, you are in an ideal position to offer whole-person care. Your God-centered perspective puts you in a unique place to treat patients' multidimensionality—factoring in culture, family background, and spiritual beliefs and hopes—as opposed to treating only their physical illness. This results in more thorough and comprehensive care. "Sure," you may say, "but shouldn't I leave spiritual issues up to the chaplain? I don't want to get involved in that sort of thing." This might seem to be the easy way out, but spiritual needs are intimately tied to a person's health. For you to offer the best care to your patient, you should address them. Even The Joint Commission didn't say anything about leaving it only up to the chaplain!

What turns many of us off is our perception of what it means to address spiritual issues. Some see it as asking something along the lines of, "Do you know Jesus Christ as your personal Lord and Savior, having been born again in the resurrective power of the Spirit?" Although such statements are well-meaning, without knowing the patient's religious background, this would probably be ineffective and even counterproductive to serving God's kingdom. Nonbelievers can be turned off by Christian jargon and may link it to feelings of negativity and oppression.

Ask yourself, "Who am I talking with? Does this person have a church background? Is he or she actively practicing his or her faith? Who or what does this person turn to in times of struggle?" We must choose our words wisely, approaching patients with permission, respect, and sensitivity, if we are to maintain open doors to be able to reach those who may be spiritually open to the Lord.

Some may wonder, *If we are ministering to people of different faiths, should we still pray in the name of Jesus?* This is something you'll have to decide in each situation. If I know the patient is of another faith, I tend to focus on God's love, patience, and sovereignty. But I still offer to pray! In fact, it's my experience that when people in emotional pain are offered the opportunity to pray, regardless of their faith background, they seldom refuse.[3] If you think that a patient would benefit from spiritual care, consider it your honor and privilege to do so. Just remember that the goal isn't to share the gospel in shotgun style just so you can check it off your list. It should be seen as just a part of whole-person care. Spiritual support can be offered just like any other medical practice. If there is a need and the patient gives consent, such care is appropriate and beneficial.[4]

There Is HOPE

While it might seem uncomfortable at first, whole-patient care includes obtaining a spiritual history. This is necessary to be certain that the whole patient, including his or her coping and support system, is being addressed. The *American Family Physician* journal published an article[5] detailing questions health-care professionals can ask their patients to assess their spiritual backgrounds and histories. There are many mnemonic devices that can aid you in doing so. Consider the simple acronym HOPE.

The HOPE Questions for a Formal Spiritual Assessment in a Medical Interview

H:	Sources of hope, meaning, comfort, strength, peace, love, and connection
	How are you finding the internal support and strength to get through this illness?
O:	Organized religion
	Are you part of a religious or spiritual community? How important is it to you?
P:	Personal spirituality and practices
	What sorts of things do you do in your practice of spirituality to help you get through tough times?
E:	Effects on medical care and end-of-life issues
	Are you concerned about anything with your medical care that would conflict with your beliefs?

If you find it difficult to know where to start when it comes to discussing a patient's spirituality (or you have concerns that you might in the future), perhaps this mnemonic will stem your apprehension. You can certainly use another mnemonic or create your own. Just use something that you feel comfortable with and that you can recall easily.

Here are some other questions I have asked and that you can consider when interviewing a patient:

- You seem fearful about what's been going on. What do you feel has scared you the most about all this?
- Can you tell me about your family? Are they involved in your life?
- Do you have any friends you can talk with about this?
- When was the last time you felt healthy?
- Are you able to make any sense out of your being ill?
- What do think this ordeal has taught you about yourself?

Sharing Our Hope

Another concern I commonly hear expressed is, "I don't think we should push our religion onto others, especially since we hold a certain position of authority as being part of the medical profession. It sounds like coercion." As a result, many believers keep silent when opportunities come their way to support someone spiritually. If this happens to you, I would encourage you to consider this: because the Christian faith is an accurate reflection of reality, the truth of the gospel does not suddenly fail in its promises or diminish in reality when you or anyone enters the hospital wards.

Some medical students believe that sharing the gospel always means presenting something akin to the four spiritual laws in booklet form. There is nothing wrong with doing this (I myself have used this method), but to believe that this encapsulates the essence of the gospel message is a misperception. The significance of Christ's death for the redemption of his people is fundamental to having a saving knowledge of God, but leaving people with the idea that the gospel means simply entering the kingdom of God and not living it out is like giving Jesus the keys to your house but telling him he needs to stay in the foyer!

Don't limit God's kingdom work. His reign and rule involve all of the rooms in your life, including those in which you interact, talk with, and care for your patients. You can actively participate in his plan for the lives of those you encounter. When you are taking a spiritual history, you may have an opportunity to simply pray for a patient's health. Or as you open up to the Spirit's leading, God may call you to share his full plan of redemption. If you feel that the Spirit is leading you in this direction, one opening question might be, "Many patients say they want to get closer to God. Would you say that is true of you?" If the patient agrees, consider following with: "For those patients who say they want to get closer to God, I am willing to explain how one might do that. Would it be helpful to you if I took a few minutes to talk more about this?"

A phenomenal opportunity in which I took part—and which I highly recommend to help you ethically and sensitively care for the whole person with the hope and gospel of Christ—is the Whole Person Care Preceptorship. This is a month-long summer missions project based in Southern California that teaches these principles to medical students and other health-care practitioners.[6]

With other patients, the Lord may be telling you to live out the gospel simply by being kind to someone who is rude or inconsiderate. He may encourage you to see the value in someone the world thinks has none—like the drunk or addict who comes to the ER every several days for detox.

If setting goals helps you express the grace and love of God to others, then consider doing that, but by no means should you be disappointed if you don't meet those goals. Your calling is to walk with Christ hour-by-hour, not to follow self-imposed guidelines to the letter (e.g., "I have to share the gospel with at least two people today!"). Guidelines are not meant to dictate the success of your walk with God. They are only meant to be an avenue by which the power of God can be manifested through your humble reliance upon him. Focus on maintaining fellowship with the Lord and walking with him step-by-step. When you do this, you are living out the gospel in front of your patients and peers around you.

Here are some other tips that may help you as you begin your patient-interviewing process.

Spend time with your patients.

In the clinical setting, for the sake of time, it is often difficult to sit down and explore nonclinical details of patients' lives. You might feel that these details won't help you diagnose the problem, so you treat the patient promptly and send him on his way. However, truly caring for patients means looking not just at the illness and the treatment but also at the person experiencing that illness. To understand the person, those so-called "irrelevant" details are important. Meaningful care—and having a meaningful connection—is one of the best investments you can make in your patients.

There is no such thing as a chance meeting.

Take opportunities to talk with patients and learn about their lives. Ask God to speak through you to each person you meet. Whether it is during your interviewing class or your rotations in the future, do not be afraid to take the time to get to know each patient in your care. As an intern or resident, you may have less time to go into a high level of detail, but you are not a resident just yet. You are a medical student. Now is the time when you have access to the hospital with the very least of responsibilities! You do not have to check up or write orders on the twenty patients on your team's service or answer your call beeper every five minutes. Take advantage of your status to spend time with your patients. You will be new at this, so naturally it will take more time, but don't rush through it. Efficiency will come with practice and effort. Focus on asking the proper questions to get the whole picture of what your patient is dealing with.

Be honest that you are a student.

There is no need or benefit to calling yourself a doctor just yet. Not only is it dishonest, but you may run into legal problems later on. Simply introduce yourself as a medical student, student doctor, or anything along those lines. Some patients may not want to talk to students for various reasons, but in my experience, many will eagerly engage you in conversation. If you approach them with a listening ear and a kind heart, they will tell you more than you ever anticipated. You will reap valuable experience as well.

Don't judge your patients.

Only God can ultimately bring judgment upon someone, and your role as a believer is to be a vessel of his mercy and grace. It can be understandably frustrating to see patients who practice self-damaging behavior and return to the hospital for the same reasons over and over again. It can be easy to condemn them, but remember that you and I also deserved condemnation. Were it not for Christ, we would still be condemned—not to mention that our very condemnation of others warrants the judgment and wrath of God. Your calling as a medical student is to learn how to care for your patients and love them as Christ loved them. Don't blame your patients, however they might seem to deserve it.

Be patient with yourself.

Some students find it hard to enjoy their initial interviewing experiences, because they find it difficult to remember all the things they have to ask. Many times, I caught myself trying to think up the next question while the patient was still answering the previous one. My goal was to prevent an embarrassing silence, but in the process, I wasn't paying attention to the patient's answer! My interviews often ended up jumbled, repetitive, and disjointed: "What? I already asked if you had problems with memory loss? Are you sure?" Even if you feel awkward with prolonged silence, realize that this is normal. Instead of beating yourself over the head for not being smooth and polished, accept your clumsy or bumbling questions with a dose of humility, and see them as great lessons to grow graciously in learning the practice of medicine.

Suggested Prayer

"Father, as I learn how to interview and examine patients, I pray for increasing wisdom and skill to learn how to care for these people you have placed before me. Thank you for the confidential privilege of being able to deal with the most intimate of issues. I pray for continued growth in being able to deal with these conversations in a professional, humble, and loving manner. I stand in thankful confidence that I am your beloved son (or daughter), and I go forth in that truth. Strengthen me and help me fight any suggestions that I am any less because of what I do or not do. Give me the courage and sense to address the spiritual backgrounds of my patients, and keep my heart sensitive to your Spirit's leading as I share the truly good news both in word and deed. Open doors and opportunities, even this week, and help me walk through them in faith."

Questions to Ponder

1. Have you ever had an uncomfortable moment when you interviewed a patient? Did you think the patient would think less of you or that you would lose his or her trust because of it?

2. When we don't know an answer to something, how does having an attitude of humility bring God honor in our interactions with patients? How is this freeing for us, especially for those who struggle with not wanting to feel embarrassed or ashamed?

3. How is keeping a patient's information in confidence a reflection of the gospel's evaluation of the person as valuable and important?

4. What is your method of asking about a patient's spiritual background? If you don't have one, consider preparing some questions before you interview your next patient and prayerfully ask God to open doors for you to connect with them in a meaningful way.

Chapter 14 Endnotes

1. The Joint Commission's paper on this topic can be downloaded here: http://www.jointcommission.org/assets/1/6/ARoadmapforHospitalsfinalversion727.pdf.

2. J. M. Milstein, "Introducing Spirituality in Medical Care," *JAMA*, Vol. 299, no. 20, 2440–2441.

3. If you would like to better understand where people with different faith backgrounds come from in order to render your spiritual care sensitively and wisely, consider reading "The Soul of Medicine: Spiritual Perspectives and Clinical Practice," edited by John R. Peteet and Michael N. D'Ambra (John Hopkins University Press, 2011).

4. *Archives of Internal Medicine,* 2007; 167:649–654. *JAMA.* 2004; 291(23). *Journal of Surgical Education,* 2011 Jan–Feb; 68(1):36–43. *Journal of General Internal Medicine,* 2011 Nov; 26(11):1265–71. *Journal of Rehabilitation Medicine,* 2011 Mar; 43(4):316–22. *Southern Medical Journal,* 2004 Dec; 97 (12).

5. Adapted or reprinted with permission from "Spirituality and Medical Practice: Using the HOPE Questions as a Practical Tool for Spiritual Assessment," *American Family Physician,* vol. 63, no. 1 (January 1, 2001). Copyright © 2001 American Academy of Family Physicians. All rights reserved.

6. More information on the Whole Person Care Preceptorship can be found here: http://www.gomets.org/student_project.html.

CHAPTER 15

Preparing for the Wards: Your First Rotations

For me, the transition from the medical classroom into the hospital wards was even more challenging than the transition from college into medical school. After countless hours sitting in lectures, working in labs, and poring over textbooks, I was suddenly thrust into the "real world" of medicine. Rather than words on a page, diseases and the people who suffered from them became tangible realities, and I had the awesome and terrifying responsibility of caring for them. Studying now occurred during rounds by the bedside and in the hospital hallway, and classes took place during morning report and noon conference. And instead of my own bed, I would soon be sleeping on the same lumpy, well-used, never-changed mattress that the first medical student who ever took call there probably slept in.

At the very start of my rotations, I realized that I needed to step up and meet the challenges of "real" medicine. Being a medical student meant learning not only patients' endless pathologies but the entire hospital dynamic as well—how to communicate with patients' families, write orders, and get along with supervising residents, all while dealing with increasing levels of fatigue and stress.

As overwhelming as it initially was, my spiritual walk during those last two years of medical school would set the foundation for my career as a full-fledged physician. Those years demanded so much of my time and physical and mental energies that I was often tempted to compromise my walk with God. Some of the hardest temptations to overcome were those that came with half-truths attached to them: "I'm so tired today. I spent everything I had yesterday at the hospital. I'll just sleep in for church. No one will really notice."

You are entering a year in which more of everything will be demanded from you. If you are not prepared for this, the potential for burnout and addicting behavior is almost inevitable. Feeling fatigued, frustrated, unloved, or unappreciated are all raw emotions that can dispose one to justifying an outlet for compromising or sinful behavior. Do any of these excuses sound familiar? "I just had a rough night of call. I'll smooth things out with some alcohol." "I'm sick of people stressing me out. I just need to surf the web and maybe stumble onto some pornographic sites. After all, I need to relax." Or "I am the lowest person on the totem pole, and I feel so out-of-control. At least I'm in control of how much I eat (or purge)." These stressors can take what seems justifiable at first and turn it into consuming addictions.

Even behaviors that are not harmful in themselves can become detrimental if taken to the extreme. The apostle Paul admonished us, "'Everything is permissible' ... but not everything is beneficial" (1 Cor. 10:23) and "Everything is permissible for me—but I will not be mastered by anything" (1 Cor. 6:12). Skipping out on Christian fellowship so you can study, for example, may seem like a small deal (or in your eyes, a good thing, because of your desire to be a respected, knowledgeable doctor), but this is when you must remind yourself why you are in medical school in the first place.

Are your intentions really to glorify God or yourself? He has made clear that we are not to give up meeting together, as some are in the habit of doing. Do you find that when the going gets tough and time

111

is short, you place your own ambitions in medicine in front of your ultimate calling to live for him? Don't push away the loving hand that offers you the physical, mental, and spiritual strength to thrive through medical school. Honor him by giving him your firstfruits, and he will honor you.

How do you go about doing this? The important thing is to set up a spiritual infrastructure for your day. No matter how polished, fancy, or impressive a building looks on the outside, without a solid foundation it will only be a matter of time before it weakens and crumples under external pressure. The infrastructure of your spiritual life is like a set of pillars that will support and provide strength for you during your day, regardless of how busy you are.

Make Quiet Time a Habit

You may have heard it said that the amount of effort you put into your rotations determines how much you will get out of them. In the same way, the more effort you put into being consistent in your quiet time with God, the more you will get out of it and the stronger your faith will be. My daily routine for spending time with God began in the mornings during breakfast. This was, of course, once I was able to formulate a coherent thought after stumbling bleary-eyed and disoriented into the shower.

Afterward, as I ate, I would go to an online daily devotional called *Our Daily Bread* or to a devotional called *My Utmost for His Highest* by Oswald Chambers. Reading a short chapter in either one and saying a short prayer usually took no more than ten minutes. Though I am not advocating a hit-and-run approach to devotions, you can still make use of what time you do have to drink from God's Word with the multitude of devotional resources available, either printed or online.

One big issue I struggled with in my devotional time was how quickly I forgot whatever I had read as I was heading out the door. Bob Mason, a minister devoted to helping Christian health-care professionals like ourselves, offers several great ideas for how to remember God's Word throughout the day:

1. Keep God's Word close to you by loading a Bible application on your smartphone or tablet so you can refer to it at any time of day. Some versions are free, such as the ESV, NAS, and NLT, and some cost only a few dollars, and can be found on websites such as www.Olivetree.com.

2. Create a daily prayer list that covers various categories (family, finances, ministry, personal petitions, prayer requests from others, etc.). You can write this in the "notes" section of your phone or tablet. When you are on a rotation that has long hours, there will be some downtime at work—waiting for labs to come back, for a callback, or for an attending to show up. Use those segments of three to five minutes to read the Bible or pray through your daily requests. Using your phone allows you to discreetly redeem that very brief downtime.

3. You can download sermons or talks from various churches or ministries from websites such as www.Oneplace.com and listen to those as you commute to work, exercise, wait for attendings, and so on.[1]

When I first started doing this, I found it surprisingly comforting. I didn't realize how powerful God's Word was, especially in the middle of the day when I was caught up in the hustle and bustle of hospital work. While it was easy to compartmentalize my spiritual life at home and my work life at the hospital, his Word was a reminder that the Holy Spirit was at work, not just in my own life but also in the lives of those around me. Remember that God is a personal and communal God. He is at work around you, even in the person sitting next to you as you read this!

Need for Christian Community

While personal communion with God is important, communion with God as part of the larger Christian community is just as important. One challenge you will face during your core rotations is the fact that being on-call during the weekends seriously limits time for fellowship and accountability. This, however, makes communion with believers all the more significant. With less fellowship comes an easier opportunity for the world to exert a negative influence on your spiritual walk.

Well-meaning medical students may begin with the desire to help the poor and heal the sick, but they often end up being influenced by the desire for a large house, a larger car, and an even larger income. You must step back regularly and ask yourself, "What am I really pursuing? Does it align with my main priority as a son or daughter of Christ, my Lord and King?"

The approval of peers and excelling in your rotations can truly be the enemy of what is best: serving Christ in humbleness and seeing his kingdom grow to fruition in our lives. If we are not careful, the lack of fellowship—combined with the insanely long work hours and the negative influence of hospital culture, with its endless demands upon our energy—will drain away our passion for God and hollow us out into hard, empty shells of what we once were. Pursue God, not the calling of God.

The Importance of Being Open

Coming from a family of doctors, I thought I was familiar with how the hospital and its doctors ran things. I had watched my dad in clinic, making rounds on his patients and interacting with the staff. I made the mistake, however, of assuming that because I had watched my father, I too knew the ins and outs of what medical students and residents were responsible for in the hospital. As a medical student myself, I constantly ran into situations in which I thought, *This isn't how I thought things were supposed to be!*

After experiencing the epically long time it took me to write a history and physical (H&P), admit a patient, and stay late to follow up on a patient, I finally realized that what had once seemed to me to be simple or easy (after all, my dad did all that without breaking a sweat—my *dad!*), really only came after much time and practice. Most of my frustration stemmed from the assumption that I would be able to assimilate into the hospital with little effort. In actuality, it required much more mental and physical energy than I realized.

This annoyed and frazzled me. What I needed to do was to approach the hospital as if I were studying a different culture in a different country, keeping my mind open and carefully observing how the attendings and residents ran things. It was then that I could see how to integrate myself into the team and offer my help, while learning medicine in the process. This really helped me begin to get a sense of the team's flow. In my pursuit of fitting in, however, I encountered another problem I had been struggling with all through medical school—living for the approval of those I tried so hard to get along with.

Suggested Prayer

"Lord, I know the hospital wards are going to be a big change for me in many respects. I don't know all the new challenges that I will face, but help me lay down a foundation with spiritual roots that will sink deeply into the rich soil of your Word. Help me establish spiritual disciplines and habits, not in my own strength but in yours, so that during the turbulent storms that come my way, my soul will be steadfastly grounded in you. Remind me of your truths as I turn to you in moments throughout the day. Please help me prioritize communing with other believers on a regular basis so I won't forget the bigger picture of your will for me. Give me an openness and humility to learn from those around me. I want to walk with you, Lord. Help me to do so today."

Questions to Ponder

1. If you have not yet begun rotations, do you feel prepared mentally and spiritually to do so?
2. What steps can you take, even this week, to keep the Lord's Word close to your heart?
3. What can you do to be reminded that God is at work in people all around you, even in the hospital and clinics?
4. How can you keep an open attitude in your interactions with those in the hospital as you begin the wards?

Chapter 15 Endnotes

1. Bob Mason, personal communication.

CHAPTER 16

Residents, Attendings, and Staff—Oh My!

During my OB-GYN rotation early in my third year, I had just spent the entire night running around the hospital with the night float, evaluating patients, observing emergency C-sections, and assisting in deliveries on the labor and delivery ward. Medical students were allowed to call it a day by 7:00 a.m., if they had been in the hospital the night before. Needless to say, as morning came, I was looking forward to heading home and getting a good dose of sleep. As I looked at my watch, I realized that it was about twenty minutes before seven, and the night float was finishing up with his duties. This hour also marked the time when the incoming medical students were required to show up for morning report, held by the residents and attending in the hospital cafeteria.

By this time, I was staying awake by sheer willpower. I was running on fumes, but a crazy thought (probably due to the lack of sleep) ran through my head. Why not stay for morning report? My heart swelled as I thought of the sacrifice of sleep I was making in order to advance my knowledge of obstetrics. After all, it wouldn't be too demanding. I would just sit in, contribute what I knew to the group, and leave inspired. Instead of saying good-bye to the night float, I lingered around.

Less than five minutes later, another resident who had just arrived came tearing around the nurse's desk and pointed at me: "You're a medical student, right?" I nodded. "Good, you'll be giving morning report today. Let me find you a patient ..." She ruffled through some papers, and with about fifteen minutes to go, I was frantically taking notes from the patient's folder, as I mentally rehearsed how I would present the case. I quickly wrote down all the labs and looked up on the computer all the dictated reports I could. As I wrote, I felt all my remaining energy drain slowly away.

At 7:00 a.m., we were in the hospital cafeteria, and I was discussing the patient. The attending peppered me with questions, which I thought I answered well. Of course, I was somewhat delirious after having been up most of twenty-four hours. As everyone was leaving after the report, the attending pulled me aside along with the resident and took me by surprise by saying, "That was the most unprepared morning report I've heard! You had all night to get ready for this. Next time, get your information and your act together." In my shock and fatigue, I couldn't argue—I really wasn't prepared—but inside I was seething. "When you get a patient," the attending continued, "you should have followed her throughout the day and studied up the night before about this particular presentation—which you obviously didn't do. I really didn't like this talk, so you should do another one. But make sure next time you go over it with me first before you present it."

I bit my lip as a part of me within screamed, "I don't even have to be here! I came out of my own goodwill. A resident accosted me to give this morning report! It's not my fault!" Here I was, being berated by an attending, when I could have been getting much-needed rest in the deep comfort of my blankets. But in the midst of waves of raw emotion, I kept my mouth shut and tried to swallow the positive aspects of his criticism, which felt like chugging a two-liter bottle of contrast. In front of my peers and several residents, I felt as if I were the one getting a pap smear!

One of the residents eventually stepped in and spoke up for me, but for me the damage was done. I trudged home, angry and exhausted. You can imagine the frustration and bitterness I felt, not just because I felt wrongly accused, but because my "image" was now tarnished, and a bad evaluation was pending! My cynicism grew. *No good deed goes unpunished*, I thought. Here I was, voluntarily staying after a tiring call in order to expand my knowledge base, only to be slammed with accusations of lack of knowledge and preparation, along with getting a potentially negative evaluation. How would you respond in such a situation? Better yet, how *should* you respond?

If you have had little exposure to being in a hospital, or you only know what you have seen on *Grey's Anatomy* or *House*, then setting foot in the hospital wards as a third-year can be intimidating and initially overwhelming. Whether you realize it or not, your idea of what a doctor is like and your growth as a medical student will be significantly influenced by those you work with—attendings, nurses, pharmacists, patients, and many others. Evaluations by residents and attendings hold sway in how you interact with them. The pressure to perform well is a very real one, and more often than not, it becomes our primary purpose: "I need to get the attending to like me so I can get a good evaluation and hopefully 'honor' this rotation so I can get into a good residency." We want to appear smart, adept at examining a patient, and able to give comprehensive differential diagnoses for a rare zebra of a disease, especially if it's in front of our residents or attendings.

While we cannot easily tell another's motivation for his or her actions, we must be careful with our own. How can we tell if our own motivations are wrong-headed—when attendings and residents become like gods to us, and we believe that their decisions ultimately determine the outcome of our future? It is often our response to crisis situations that reveals where our hope truly lies and challenges us about whom we really trust with our future.

As I look back years later, I find it humorous that my initial reason for staying for morning report was because of an eager yet prideful desire to go the extra mile so others would take notice and be impressed. I knew it was prideful, because as my time there went from an enjoyable learning experience to a medical student's horror story, my visceral response to my attending welled up from self-righteous anger. It did not reflect my calling as a medical student who was learning to walk in humility.

So what should be the proper attitude and motivation toward our attendings, residents, and staff? What do you do with the hierarchy seen on some rotations or the malignant personalities displayed by some attendings and residents—especially when they are the ones evaluating you? Is the proper Christian response to meekly submit, "for you shall inherit the earth," or to boldly defy your superiors, citing Romans 8:31, "If God is for us, who can be against us"? What should our response be when we don't live up to the expectations of those evaluating us?

Not all situations have a clear-cut "this is what God taught me" lesson. Some situations—especially when they come out of the blue—can be traumatic to the point where all we can do is open our mouths and shake our heads in disbelief. When you feel unjustly treated, Jesus is there with you in that experience, understanding the multitude of emotions you may not be able to put into words. Not only is he with you, but he is sovereignly powerful to guide and protect you. He isn't caught by surprise by what just happened. In fact, in his sovereign wisdom, he ordained it. I know this is a hard saying, but God's love is often a tough love. This is where knowledge of God's sovereignty becomes more than just academic theology. God's sovereignty becomes your very source of comfort and hope. You need to trust him with your circumstance, even though you may not know the reason why you are going through your particular suffering.

What We Fear Reflects What We Value

As a third-year medical student, you likely feel that you are on the low end of the totem pole in the hierarchy of the hospital academic system. As a result, you may find that you have the tendency to gauge how well your day went by whether the resident or attending you worked with treated you well. This is especially true when you are on rotations that demand a significant amount of energy and time. With tiredness come testy nerves. Was I yelled at that day? Was I able to impress the attending with my fund of knowledge? Did he or she like the presentation I gave? Why do I feel inept in front of my smarter peers? Why do I fear the sneer of the peer?

There are generally two ways students approach their interactions with their attendings. One is characterized by the need to constantly please. Whether it is simply to "get the grade" or just to stay away from any sense of disapproval, not wanting to be looked down upon is a powerful impetus for doing well.

The second approach is the opposite: it involves throwing anyone's negative opinions of you out the window and not giving any thought to what others think—all that matters is what you know, your own sense of pride, and your own self-respect. In my experience, this is rare, because medical students seem to inherently understand that they come from a position of knowing less and having limited experience compared to attendings, residents, and even fourth-year students. Students know that ignoring correction from more experienced clinicians can compromise patient care and lead to bad outcomes. I think most students are somewhere in between. They want to be confident in their own personal growth in medicine, yet they are willing to go the extra mile to be looked upon by their attendings in a favorable light.

How can you achieve a healthy balance in a way that is God-glorifying so that you are neither a walking doormat nor stubbornly unteachable?

Personality differences aside, how well you interact with those above you in the medical hierarchy is directly related to the source from which you derive your self-worth. Do you find your worth in how well you absorb medical facts and score on exams? How about recognition by others of your intellectual and mental capacity? If so, what do you do when an attending berates you for your lack of understanding? Is there an inward response of anger from damaged pride and a desire to prove yourself "worthy," especially in front of other students? Does it become your driving goal to please others until you finally feel validated? Or do you respond to correction with avoidance of that particular attending or involve yourself in unhealthy habits to escape feelings of failure? If your response leans toward either furious internal anger or timid emotional withdrawal, both are indications that you have wrongly placed your hope and self-worth in the opinions of others.

Robert McGee, a Christian counselor and author, powerfully describes the incredible futility of doing such a thing:

> Isn't it amazing that we turn to others who have a perspective as limited and darkened as our own to discover our worth! Rather than relying on God's steady, uplifting reassurance of who we are, we depend on others who base our worth on our ability to meet their standards. Because our performance and ability to please others so dominate our search for significance, we have difficulty recognizing the distinction between our real identity and the way we behave, a realization crucial to understanding our true worth. Our true value is not based on our

behavior or the approval of others but on what God's Word says is true of us. If we base our worth solidly on the truths of God's Word, then our behavior will often reflect his love, grace, and power. But if we base our worth on our abilities or the fickle approval of others, then our behavior will reflect the insecurity, fear, and anger that come from such instability ... The desire for success and approval constitutes the basis of an addictive, worldly self-worth. If we base our self-worth on the approval of others, then we are actually saying that our ability to please others is of greater value than Christ's payment.[1]

Don't take another person's fallen, sinfully limited opinion of you over the omniscient God's declaration of who you really are. Remind yourself daily that, because of Christ's death and resurrection, you are completely forgiven, wholly loved, and incredibly valued by the God of the universe. God is not a temperamental attending who pretends to be a good-natured teacher one day and then seethes with burning criticism the next. Christ already died for the punishment you deserved. You are no longer under any judgment or condemnation. God's love for you is ever constant, never changing, and will always be there to give you strength and hope.

As much as some attendings hate to admit it, they are not God. Their value and opinion of you should only be allowed for the purpose of edification in your medical education, and no more. Too often, we become engrossed in seeking to please our attendings' every whim, cringing at their slightest frown or shrinking at their smallest hint of disapproval. We become consumed by getting a good evaluation because, after all, how else will we be able to improve our chances of getting into a competitive residency? If we get into a good residency, then we will have a good chance of getting into a good fellowship, and then our life will be complete!

Do you really think that the resident/attending/chief/advisor you are trying to please has the power to ultimately determine your destiny? Your answer to that reveals whether you are really trusting in Christ or in man's approval of you. There is a difference between honoring those above you and skyrocketing them to godlike status (which, simply put, is idolatry). Not all residents or attendings are looking out for your well-being or best interest, so why fear them, let them intimidate you, or let them become the focus of your well-being?

It is not the singular, driving purpose of your resident or attending to give you glowing praises or to bestow honor on you. As much as you want to, don't seek it out. Your attendings and residents are there to encourage your learning. Whether they do it in a kind way or a rude way, don't take it personally. They all come from different places, and your goal is to learn and work well with them. Once they see that you are working in a manner pleasing to the Lord, then out of that witness can birth a positive outlook and evaluation. Even if this is not the case, refuse to believe that this single, finite person can change the course of your life.

If you live to give the omnipresent, holy, and all-powerful Christ glory, then he will lift you up. God is in control here. No matter what your attendings, residents, or colleagues say, honor God first, and he will honor you. It is important to learn this now, or else you will be stuck trying to get the approval of others, even after medical school is done. In residency you will be trying to please your attendings, and after residency you will be wanting the approval of your colleagues … and on and on. Colossians 3:23–24 says, "Whatever you do, work at it with all your heart, as working for the Lord, not for human masters, since you know that you will receive an inheritance from the Lord as a reward. It is the Lord Christ you are serving."

Learn from your attendings as your mentors and teachers with a humble, open mind, but give your heart only to the Great Attending, the one who truly cares for you and determines that you, by the blood of Christ, are fully worthy.

Christ's Calling as Motivation to Care

If we shouldn't be consumed by what our attendings think of us, then what motivation do we have to treat patients or to learn how to care for the sick? Is there not a natural tendency to slack off and simply look for the easiest route through medical school? Do I really need to spend more time at the hospital, burning the midnight oil, especially if it doesn't matter what others may think of me? Could I just do the bare minimum, as long as I pass?

Dr. Harvey Elder offers sage advice for how to approach your professional calling: "[Your] goals are not self-referenced. That is, they do not include convenience, hours, income, status, rewards, and so on."[2] In other words, leave your conveniences, comforts, and other thoughts on how little you can do to get by, and focus instead on what God has called you to do in this ministry of healing. Dr. Elder continues: "Ours is a ministry to the sick, hurt and dying. That is, we, as God's called servants, serve his hurting children. Our priorities, goals and actions are those of service. The multiple aspects and implications of our patient's specific circumstances, history and manifestations present challenges to surmount as we seek to serve them."[3]

Our work will require much effort, both in the comprehensiveness of what we need to learn and in the synthesis of it. But remember that success is a function of being engaged, not of determining your outcomes. Your satisfaction should be found in engaging yourself wholly with your patients, residents, and attendings, not on whether you are impressing your supervisors enough to get an honors grade.

Let the call of Christ in the ministry of healing be your motivation for taking extra steps in caring for your patients.

Out of his loving heart, Christ went to the cross for your sins that you might be brought from a hopeless state to one of healing, so consider it a joyful motivation to serve your patients in the same manner that Christ served you. Robert McGee writes: "Although we may expend tremendous effort at great personal cost, only that which is done for Christ's glory in the power of His Spirit is of eternal value."[4] Serve your team and your patients for Christ's glory, and trust that God will be magnified and glorified in amazing ways.

Suggested Prayer

"Father, thank you that you know exactly who I am. Thank you that you love me in spite of my shortcomings. I confess that sometimes in my anger or frustration, I doubt your goodness to me, and sometimes these trials don't seem to make any sense. Help me to trust you regardless, simply because I know you are sovereign, holy, and truly good. Give me the wisdom and grace to listen to and learn from my attendings, but not for them to replace you. I worship you alone. Lord, my calling is to serve the sick and the hurt, so help me not to slack off, but instead engage my work with all my effort so that you may be glorified in it!"

Questions to Ponder

1. Describe a time when you felt you were unjustly treated or unfairly judged by your peers, resident, or attending. How does your response to that particular situation reveal the character that is in you?

2. How can the sovereignty of God help refocus you when you are faced with such situations?
3. In addition to God's sovereignty, how can the strong, persistent, and powerful love of God re-center you?
4. As you learn how to heal others, think of ways you can engage yourself in medical school by reflecting on the healing that Christ gave you.

Chapter 16 Endnotes

1. Robert McGee, *Search for Significance* (Nashville: Thomas Nelson, 2003), 19, 74.
2. Dr. Harvey Elder, personal communication.
3. Dr. Harvey Elder, personal communication.
4. *Search for Significance*, 129.

CHAPTER 17

Taking Call ... and Giving It Back

After you get your clinical rotation schedule—whether you start off with psychiatry, surgery, or anything else—your thoughts will eventually wander to the day labeled "On Call." Perhaps, like me, you might envision your expectations of a typical night.

You set your backpack down in the call room. Abruptly, the pager clipped to your waist emits its characteristic shrill squawk—and you're off to admit your first patient! On the way, the resident turns to you and says, "Why don't you head down to the emergency department first? I'll meet you there in a little bit."

As you make a beeline to the ED, maybe a bit excited (and definitely a bit nervous), the overhead page interrupts everyone's attention: "Code blue ... floor 2, room 289, code blue ..." A stat emergency! You hold off admitting the patient and run to the code, as you see other residents in blue scrubs sprinting past you. In their midst is your resident, whose normally calm demeanor is betrayed by a look of worry in her eye and a glistening forehead, as she tries to keep up with the surgical interns while keeping her smartphone and papers from flying out of her pocket.

Suddenly the overhead blares: "Code red, floor 2 ..." A fire! You note that even the overhead operator's voice seems more urgent and stressed than before. As you burst onto the floor, you see nurses screaming in panic, holding their arms up around a raging fire at the nurse's station, while a helpless intern frantically shouts, "Does anyone know where the defibrillator is? *Where is the defibrillator?*" Suddenly the lights and electricity in the entire hospital shut off, and everyone is engulfed in a stifling sea of smoke and blackness.

When you come back to reality, you realize that you're clutching your call schedule a little too tightly.

The vast majority of medical students most likely won't experience anything like this, at least not all at the same time. In fact, it sounds more like a typical rerun of *ER* or *House*. In reality, you will find that the emergency room has likely stabilized the patient you will be admitting, so if an emergency arises, you know that the patient will still be taken care of while he or she waits in the ED. Codes do occur, but more often than not, you won't be the first to arrive there, and you won't be the one running them. (The codes are run by residents and attendings.)

And the fire alarm? In my experience, most of the time the alarm is cancelled within five minutes, because someone was trying to sneak a smoke in the bathroom. This is not to say that you should casually ignore codes or fire alarms. Follow the hospital's protocol, but don't panic!

There are certain challenges that occur when taking call, but as you will discover, call nights present unique opportunities for Christian medical students to minister to patients, fellow colleagues, and even themselves.

Why Does Taking Call Seem So Hard?

Medical students and residents have difficulty stomaching their call schedules for a multitude of reasons. Taking call mixes up your sleep schedule, leaving many mentally and physically worn out the next day. It requires a measure of physical stamina in order to deal with long stretches of time without sleep. It also demands that you have the mental acuity necessary during times of physical stress and tiredness to make the decisions that are best for the patient. It also, by nature, keeps you from spending time with friends and family.

While taking call can be very challenging, I have found that there are some advantages as well, particularly in your role as being the very hands and heart of Christ to your patients and fellow colleagues.

Take the Time

It's too easy to hide in the call room with the intern or resident, dreading the next page. Why not take a walk around the hospital instead? I don't mean to familiarize yourself with the hospital's building structure—although at first you may have to do just that. With the permission of your supervising resident, why not check up on a patient you are taking care of? When the hustle and bustle of writing orders, calling in consults, or checking labs starts to wind down, consider taking some time to interact with patients, especially when they least expect you. Even a simple "hello" brings warmth to those who are often left alone in a sterile environment. Some say, "That's a job for the nurses," but since when has simple compassion or kindness been confined to the nurse's job description? If you think in terms of the nurses showing compassion while the doctors treat only the physical disease, you have failed to appreciate the incredible complexity of human nature, wherein God has created us all in his image.

Like a sparkling diamond, a person is of one essence, but he is multifaceted in the expression of that essence. There are many sides to us—social, spiritual, physical, and mental—so merely treating the physical aspect actually under-treats the patient you have been given the privilege and responsibility of caring for. Patients and their families experience comfort and healing from your willingness to lend a listening ear and speak calming words into their unease.

As an intern, I once received a page from a harried nurse who asked me to see a daughter who was worried that her father was in a lot of pain. I came up to the floor, and after reviewing the patient's chart and examining him, I had the feeling that the only person in real distress was the daughter! I sat her down and explained that her father was not in pain and that we would watch him carefully overnight to make sure he remained that way. After several minutes, she became visibly relieved and was able to go home in much better shape than when she'd arrived.

As I walked over to the nursing station, I relayed to the nurse what I told the daughter, and to my surprise, the nurse threw up her hands in dismay. "That's exactly what I told her!" The clue as to why the daughter responded the way she did were in her words to me before she left: "I trust you because you're the doctor." By sheer virtue of our role in the hospital, whether we are a medical student, a resident, or an attending, we are inherently granted a level of trust (deserved or undeserved) from our patients and those close to them. From our "high" position (being responsible and taking care of patients) and interacting with them in their "low" position (those who are sick and need our help), we become a spiritual reflection of Jesus himself, who humbled himself so that we, the sick, might be redeemed and healed.

I am not saying that we are God to those we treat. Rather, if we meditate on the incredibly compassionate character of Jesus as he looked at the downtrodden, the sick, and the hungry, we can realize just what a privilege it is for us to be able to minister to those who desperately need—through us—the loving, gracious, and humble touch of Christ.

Time with the Residents

Most likely, you will be spending a lot of your call time with the residents. On the days when the service is not that busy or the ED is not humming with admissions, you can use the downtime as a prime opportunity to get to know them better. Remember this: although some residents may not act like it, they were in your shoes only a couple of years ago! Find out who they are and what makes them tick. You are part of a team, and along with trying to learn as much as you can from them, one of your goals should be to learn how to serve your teammates in a humble manner that honors Christ.

Remember that Jesus, despite being God in his very nature, stooped to our level to meet us where we were. He washed his disciples' feet. He died for us, when we deserved nothing but punishment. His whole life was an act of loving, humble service. So next time a resident turns to you in the midst of your rotations and asks you to run out and pick up some takeout for his dinner, don't grumble about being the lackey! Remember Christ's radical example of servanthood, and dare to do it joyfully, knowing that your service to people—and ultimately to the Lord—will not go unnoticed by God.

"Whether you eat or drink"—or get extra napkins for the call team, because the noodles in the call room are getting out of hand—do it "unto the Lord." Whatever you do for the Lord truly has lasting, eternal value.

Admitting Your Patient

Whenever I was given the opportunity to write up a history and physical for a patient I was admitting, I was told to take as long as I needed ... or at least until the patient's patience gave out. Taking a thorough history is important to taking care of a patient well. Some hospitals give you templates on which to do an H&P, while others may give you the (dreaded) blank sheet that you have to fill out entirely by yourself. If your hospital is one of the latter, one thing you can do is come up with a template of your own. Save it on your smartphone, or print it out and carry it with you so you can easily refer to it. This way, you know you have covered all the important details, including, for example, the history of the present illness, past medical and surgical history, spiritual background, smoking and drug history, and so on.

Taking Care of Yourself

A lack of sleep, compounded by not being able to be in your own bed, can make the day after call seem like a haze. With recent resident work-hour changes, the amount of sleep one can get has improved, but when you are so focused on helping others, it is too easy to ignore your own body's need for rest.

It is ironic that medical students and residents need to be taught about sleep debt and its effects. In fact, the Accreditation Council for Graduate Medical Education (ACGME) requires all the residencies to set aside time to talk about this.[1] Medical students who are first exposed to being on-call don't realize the toll it can take on their bodies.

Here are a few reminders that will help you understand how a lack of sleep can affect your body:

1. There is such a thing as "sleep debt."
2. The average adult needs around eight hours of sleep per night.
3. If you get less than this, your body needs to make up for the lack of sleep—hence "sleep *debt*."
4. It is a myth that your body can get used to less sleep over time. I knew someone who slept only four hours a night for one year during college. Interestingly, when she went to medical school, she could not function unless she slept at least seven hours. She *had* to sleep that much. Your body will accumulate debt, and if it isn't paid, your body will suffer.
5. "Suffering" involves increased numbers of medical errors by residents. Studies have shown that residents with sleep debt misread more EKGs, take superfluous steps and require longer time to complete procedures, and have increased failure rates in placing catheters such as arterial lines. There are also well-known cases of residents causing serious injuries and even death to others or themselves after falling asleep at the wheel the day after a grueling call.
6. The effect of caffeine kicks in about fifteen to thirty minutes after drinking coffee, the half-life of caffeine being about three to five hours. Before you go home from call, either consider drinking something with caffeine in it or first taking a nap at the hospital.
7. Your circadian rhythm makes the ideal time for your nap (if possible) to fall between 2:00 to 5:00 p.m. and 2:00 to 5:00 a.m. These times are most in tune with your body, and you get more rest that way.
8. Naps should not exceed twenty to thirty minutes. Otherwise, sleep inertia can occur. Sleep inertia is extreme grogginess

and disorientation that can last up to ten minutes, with residual symptoms lasting up to two hours.

This has happened to me. After waking from a two-hour nap in the call room, I was oblivious to where I was and made no sense to those around me. For fun, one medical resident I knew was recorded on the phone after waking up from a prolonged nap, muttering, "Some people just, nothing really, just a lot of people thinking that, um, joint pain, is what … okay, everything turned to me, that's cool … Wah!" Thankfully, he was not on call! It was quite funny when I first heard it, but imagine if there had been a nurse on the other end of the line! We can't always avoid sleep debt, but remember that there are steps we can take to keep its detrimental and sometimes serious effects to a minimum.

Consider that taking call is not a burden but an opportunity to serve the Lord. Pray for a daily realization that your life is not your own and that you belong to God, who asks for radical service of your time and energy to advance his purposes and his glory to the world around you. Then go forth and be his light!

Suggested Prayer

"Lord, I know that taking call can be really challenging. It stretches my physical stamina, tests my mind, and challenges my interactions with people. Give me your strength when I am on call. Help me be a servant to everyone you place in front of me. Let Christ be my example as I work with my call team, because ultimately I am serving you. I pray that my call will be an opportunity to give you glory. I pray that you would restore me when call is over. Help me to be wise in getting rest. Whatever happens, God, let me remember that you are in control of all things that come to pass. In the midst of my frustrations and anxieties, successes and joys, be glorified, Lord. All I do is for you."

Questions to Ponder

1. If you haven't taken call yet, what do you imagine your first night of call will be like?
2. How can you prepare yourself physically, emotionally, spiritually, and intellectually for the potential challenges?
3. What things can you do to help your team when you take call?
4. What things can you do to minister to your patients?
5. What things can you do to take care of yourself, especially after taking call?

Chapter 17 Endnotes

1. The ACGME (The Accreditation Council for Graduate Medical Education) sets guidelines and standards for residency programs in the United States. It requires residency programs to educate residents to recognize the signs of fatigue and sleep deprivation, as well as alertness management and fatigue mitigation processes. You can download the guidelines at http://www.acgme.org/acgmeweb/Portals/0/dh_dutyhoursCommonPR07012007.pdf.

CHAPTER 18

A Dark World

Blessed is the man who fears the Lord, who
finds great delight in his commands ...
He will have no fear of bad news; his heart
is steadfast, trusting in the Lord.
—Psalm 112:1, 7

The hospital becomes like a second home, simply because of the amount of time you will spend there during your training. Just like growing up in a home with parents and siblings, "growing up" as a doctor in the hospital environment can have a significant influence on the way you develop, not just as a student but as a whole person. Acute or critical care areas—like the operating room, emergency department, or intensive care unit—can be havens for stressed and overworked providers, who can pass their negative thoughts and emotions on to you.

It takes a lot of time and energy to refine your skills in medicine, and this can be emotionally and physically draining. Be careful! With a spiritual, physical, and emotional tank running on empty, a heart of bitterness can emerge. If you are not prepared to battle it, bitterness eventually can give birth to cynicism. For example, you may have heard colleagues muttering something like, "By now, my college friends are probably enjoying themselves on the weekends, making money, and working normal hours. Here I am, stuck in this foxhole, trying to get along with the residents and eating hospital food!" Sooner than you think, those lofty goals of helping the sick and caring for the weak become faded memories, replaced by feelings of cynicism and self-pity.

Medical school can be a fiery crucible for testing your spiritual fortitude. The difficulty of dealing with patients, physical tiredness, and mental pressure—especially with the lack of time to connect with a community of believers—can easily pound one into cynical submission. For some of us—before entering medical school—seeing a sick or lonely person would elicit a deep, empathetic response. But in an ironic twist—*after* medical school—this can be replaced with more unhealthy emotions if we are not careful. The very place where healing should take place is the same place where our hearts and souls can be damaged and compassion can be replaced with cynicism.

Jesus reminds us of the only place we can put our hearts in order be free from the world's power of negativity and weariness: "Store up for yourselves treasures in heaven, where moth and rust do not destroy, and where thieves do not break in and steal. For where your treasure is, there your heart will be also" (Matt. 6:20–21). By living for him, we get the ability to fight bitterness and negativity and the strength to persevere in hope.

How can we fight the sweeping currents of sinfulness and negativity seen in hospital culture? Here are several steps.

1. Believe that God is guiding your steps, both lovingly and sovereignly.

Adoniram Judson was a missionary in the 1800s who spent over forty years in Burma. In the midst of challenging setbacks, personal sacrifices, and imprisonment, Judson penned these words: "If I had not felt certain that every additional trial was ordered by infinite love and mercy, I could not have survived my accumulated sufferings."[1] In other words, his suffering was meaningful and worth struggling through, because it was ordained by a sovereign and loving God.

Christians like Judson (and you) go through real trials and real difficulties. Medical students in particular know that every day is not a pie-in-the-sky experience. That is why you must firmly cling, as Judson did, to God's infinite love and mercy despite the fires of your life experience. Helen Keller was once asked if there was anything worse than being blind. She answered, "Yes, having sight, but no vision."[2] We must keep this eternal-minded vision, lest we get caught up in the embittered mind-set that befalls many physicians.

This truth came to me in a powerful way on my night float rotation during my intern year. Night float involved taking sign-outs from the residents who were leaving for the day and admitting any patients that night. Around four in the morning, after finishing an admission from the ED, I quickly headed over to the call room to get some rest. Since my schedule was already flip-flopped (sleeping during the day and working at night), I decided to turn on the television in the call room and let time pass by. In my half-dazed state, I flipped to a channel showing the World Championship Poker Competition. The competition had reached the point at which the final table of competitors was to be determined after one more person was knocked out. And whom did I see, staring at a handful of cards? My high-school classmate!

Back in the day, we had taken many classes together. Sometimes people got us mixed up. We both were labeled as nerds and geeks, but we didn't mind. We wore those badges proudly. After classes, we'd walk to the parking lot and talk about everything—classes, sports, girls, and the gospel.

My classmate wasn't a Christian, but he was curious about my faith. There was a time during which, for two weeks each day after class, he would spend about an hour asking me questions about faith and Jesus, and asking, "How do you really know?" He even came to youth group several times. After what I can only describe as a prompting by the Spirit, I told him, "I know we both agree that I've answered a lot of your questions about God in a reasonable way, but you have to realize that I can't force you or magically talk you into becoming a Christian. You have to make that decision willingly, on your own." Though I had invited him to accept Christ, he still resisted. I soon realized that he was asking questions, not for the sake of knowing the truth, but simply for the sake of asking questions.

It was strange seeing him on TV that night. In high school, he had been shy, and sometimes people liked to make fun of him. Now, there he was, vying for the final table in the World Poker Championships. I'm not a fan of gambling, but in that moment, as my eyes locked onto his in my sleep-inertia–induced state, I asked myself, "What in the world am I doing? There he is, probably making tens or maybe even hundreds of thousands of dollars—with the potential to win millions—and fans are probably throwing themselves at him. And here I am at four o'clock in the morning, waiting for a pager to screech into my ear and tell me where to go and what to do next."

At that moment, I realized what I had done. I wasn't just being a grumpy intern. I was being deeply unfaithful. God's watchful providence had covered every single detail of my life up to the very minute that I was doubting his goodness in the solitude of that call room. Does God really care about the minutiae of my life? How could I remind myself that I really wasn't in the wrong profession and that my choices mattered to him? I don't think I have been the only person to think such things.

In fact, this was an issue that James 4:13–16 (ESV) addressed to God's people, thousands of years ago. "Come now, you who say, 'Today or tomorrow we will go into such and such a town and spend a year there and trade and make a profit'—yet you do not know what tomorrow will bring. What is your life? For you are a mist that appears for a little time and then vanishes. Instead you ought to say, 'If the Lord wills, we will live and do this or that.' As it is, you boast in your arrogance. All such boasting is evil."

Pastor John Piper once noted, "A man simply says, 'I'm driving up to Duluth for Christmas.' And James says, 'Don't be so sure.' Instead, say (v. 15), 'If the Lord wills, we shall live and we shall go to Duluth for Christmas.'"[3] God is sovereign over what we think are simple, ordinary choices in life. Remember the true words found in Proverbs 16:9: "In his heart a man plans his course, but the Lord determines his steps." In other words, everything in our lives is accounted for and sovereignly cared for by a holy and loving God—yes, even our mistakes. How freeing that truth was for me! That meant I could rest in him, knowing that because my future was entrusted to him, it was secure. I was right where God wanted me to be.

I finished watching the show. My classmate had a Jack/10, but the other player had an Ace/Queen, and on the flop, the other player won with a pair of aces and queens. I said a silent prayer for my friend and changed the channel.

Encouragement from the Word

Some verses below may help you as you meditate on them throughout your rotations. May they remind you of the Lord's call and his goodness for your life:

"As obedient children, do not conform to the evil desires you had when you lived in ignorance. But just as he who called you is holy, so be holy in all you do; for it is written: 'Be holy, because I am holy'" (1 Peter 1:14–16).

"Therefore, there is now no condemnation for those who are in Christ Jesus, because through Christ Jesus the law of the Spirit who gives life has set you free from the law of sin and death" (Rom. 8:1–2).

"For we are God's handiwork, created in Christ Jesus to do good works, which God prepared in advance for us to do" (Eph. 2:10).

"Therefore, as God's chosen people, holy and dearly loved, clothe yourselves with compassion, kindness, humility, gentleness and patience" (Col. 3:12).

"I have been crucified with Christ and I no longer live, but Christ lives in me. The life I now live in the body, I live by faith in the Son of God, who loved me and gave himself for me" (Gal. 2:20).

2. Remember that you are ultimately serving Christ, not your patient.

Even as a Christian, you are not automatically immune to cynicism or self-pity. No matter how lofty your goals or how perfect your plan to get through medical school, you must realize that the power of cynicism can affect an unwary believer. The excitement of eventually being called "doctor" and the opportunity to help the ill was my mind's-eye picture of what I would be doing. But once in the trenches of hospital life, the magical aura of medicine began to disappear. I was constantly faced with real patients who, admittedly, didn't look or smell clean, didn't care about my attempts to help them, and ignored my questions and concerns, while perseverating instead on the next time they could step outside the hospital for a smoke.

Capturing perfectly this ironic contrast between the romantic desire to help people and the realities of *actually* helping people was the Russian author Fyodor Dostoyevsky in his classic novel *The Brother's Karamazov*. In it, the Elder, a monk, describes a conversation he had with a doctor:

> "[A] certain medical man once told me, long ago now," the Elder observed … "I love mankind," he said, "but I marvel at myself: the more I love mankind in general, the less I love human beings in particular, separately, that is, as individual persons. In my dreams," he said, "I would often arrive at fervent plans of devotion to mankind and might very possibly have gone to the Cross for human beings, had that been suddenly required of me, and yet I am unable to spend two days in the same room with someone else, and this I know from experience. No sooner is that someone else close to me than his personality crushes my self-esteem and hampers my freedom. In the space of a day and a night I am capable of coming to hate even the best of human beings: one because he takes too long over dinner, another because he has a cold and is perpetually blowing his nose. I become the enemy of others," he said, "very nearly as soon as they come into contact with me. To compensate for this however, it has always happened that the more I have hated human beings in particular, the more ardent has become my love for mankind in general."[4]

Dostoyevsky's observation on human character rings true. On rotations, I have experienced horrendous halitosis from elderly patients, and manually disimpacted people suffering severe constipation. One time I needed to call the plumber to get the toilet to flush after seeing the porcelain bowl in all its glorious fullness after a patient's experience with extra strong laxatives. (Mind you, I did not want to see the toilet in the first place, but the nurse insisted!) It was during these rotations that I realized, despite my lofty longings to "help people," how truly earthy, of-the-soil, and downright human we all are. Yet here is the amazing thing: Jesus died for people like these— the foul-smelling, stool-retaining, toilet-clogging, brokenhearted sinners.

Before we distance ourselves from a particular patient, we must realize that this patient is like us. We were once spiritually sick and without hope. The spiritual stench of death that entered God's nostrils came from our wretched, rotten state that no physical smell could compare to. We could not save ourselves, but God, the Great Physician, came and brought us from the judgment of death to a life of abundant grace.

As a medical student, you now have the opportunity to offer this same supernatural patience, thoughtfulness, and love to those patients under your care. We cannot love others in our own strength (or at least not for very long), but we can ask daily for his Spirit to fill and give us the strength, wisdom, and love of God for others. Not only will he give us the energy to do this, but we can let our hearts be motivated by his words: "I tell you the truth, whatever you did for one of the least of these brothers of mine, you did for me" (Matt. 25:40). This gives us deep joy, knowing that our work, no matter how seemingly trivial or menial, has true eternal significance, because we are serving Christ himself.

Mother Teresa once said, "When we handle the sick and the needy, we touch the suffering body of Christ, and this touch will make us heroic; it will make us forget the repugnance and the natural tendencies in us. We need the eyes of deep faith to see Christ in the broken body and dirty clothes under which the most beautiful one among the sons of men hides. We shall need the hands of Christ to touch these bodies wounded by pain and suffering."[5] In relying on Christ, we are to love them as Christ loves them.

3. See your patients with the inherent value God has given them.

As a medical student, your role on the team is different from the resident's. There are some administrative nuances that the residents must learn in order to improve the flow of their hospital work, but your role is primarily to learn how best to care for the patient. Your position is not that of a glorified vending machine, responding to punched-in lab values and dispensing diagnoses and medications. Instead of getting the bare bones of what you need in order to put together a diagnosis or treatment plan, dig deeper and try to see patients as Christ sees them—as valuable, dearly loved people.

Dr. Margaret Brand, a missionary in India, said of the lepers she treated (and this is true of all people) that "the recognition of their value in the eyes of God and in their fellow men is as healing as anything we might offer in terms of medical, surgical or other professional care."[6] Unlike the doctor in Dostoyevsky's novel, we can see the beauty and the incredible value of the broken and sick through the power and eyes of the Holy Spirit.

4. Consider a domestic mission or overseas rotation during your fourth year.

The constant barrage of cynicism in the hospital—and patients who continue their bad health behaviors, despite our best efforts—tend to nurture the thorny seeds of resentment and bitterness that creep into our lives. Try thinking outside of the box: consider a rotation in an inner city or a medical mission abroad.

Dr. David Stevens, the CEO of CMDA, once recounted: "I remember doctors coming to where I worked in Kenya, and a few days after they arrived, telling me how reinvigorated they were because they 'weren't worried about being sued, not concerned about being paid, people really appreciated them, and they were saving lives physically and spiritually every day.'"

We become refreshed and rejuvenated when we give without expecting anything in return. As an added benefit, students who have gone on rotations like these have said that it is also a great place to get procedural experience. Give it a try. It might just change your heart and let you see the hospital in a whole new light! The CMDA website (www.cmda.org) has links for scholarship resources (click on the "Missions" tab on their website, and then on "Scholarships"), as well as an online manual for students, with over one hundred hospitals overseas that offer accredited rotations (click on "Missions" tab, then "Center for Medical Missions," then "Student Missions Opportunity Booklet").

5. Follow the Great Attending's example of compassion.

During my residency, as I was taking a patient from the preoperative area (where patients are kept before they are wheeled off to the operating room), the patient's daughter, who looked to be in her thirties, glared at me and blurted out: *"Banzai!"* Being of Asian descent, I was at first taken aback. Did she assume I was Japanese? Did she scream Japanese words to every Asian person she met? Nonetheless, I nervously laughed it off. I gave her the benefit of the doubt, thinking she was trying to say something to the effect of, "Let's get going! We've been waiting too long!" Perhaps to her credit, she looked shocked, as if she couldn't believe what she had just said.

It was then that the patient's other daughter, probably in her forties, piped up: "You look like someone young who's trying to look older!" Great! The dynamic duo of racism and ageism stood right before me. I was not entirely sure what she meant by that, since I was wearing the standard blue scrubs and cap everyone else wore. I cracked a smile and replied, "Wow! No one's ever told me that before." I also wanted to add, "Ladies, you're really not making it any easier to take care of your mother!"

For whatever reason, certain patients may get you irked. Even if your fellow students insist on the validity of your "righteous" anger ("You don't have to take that from her! If she's going to treat you like that, she doesn't deserve to be treated!"), remember that Christ's calling is much higher than our own internal scale of justice. We are called to love the unlovable, pray for those who persecute us, do good to those who speak evil of us, and humble ourselves, as Christ did, to serve the undeserving. This is the grace that was given to you and me, even though in our blindness we often don't see ourselves in the position of needing grace all that much. There really is a correlation between being a grace-receiver (and receiving it gladly) and a grace-giver (and giving it gladly).

Conversely, Jesus did not mean for us to just let things slide either. If a person is doing something wrong, we still need to offer correction, but not in selfish anger. We need to keep grace a priority in our lives so that we can offer it to others.

What about the patient who doesn't care about his own health? Why bother? More than once, I've heard physicians gripe, "Why help them? They're just going to go right back to what they've been doing (drinking alcohol *in extremis*, chain-smoking, injecting illicit drugs, maintaining poor control of their diet, being noncompliant with their blood pressure medications, and so on)." Indeed, why bother to heal the ungrateful sinner who will choose only to sin again?

Max Lucado provides an insightful answer to this question:

> Matthew writes that Jesus "healed their sick." Not some of their sick. Not the righteous among the sick. Not the deserving among the sick. But "the sick." Surely, among the many thousands, there were a few people unworthy of good health.
>
> The same divinity that gave Jesus the power to heal also gave him the power to perceive ... And he could see not only their past, he could see their future.
>
> Undoubtedly, there were those in the multitude who would use their newfound health to hurt others. Jesus released tongues that would someday curse. He gave sight to eyes that would lust. He healed hands that would kill ... Most would be more concerned with being healthy than being holy, but he healed them anyway. Some of those who asked for bread today would cry for his blood a few months later, but he healed them anyway ... He chose to give gifts to people, knowing full well that those gifts could be used for evil ... Each time Jesus healed, he had to overlook the future and the past. Something, by the way, that he still does ... Have you noticed that God doesn't ask you to prove that you will put your salary to good use? Have you noticed that God doesn't turn off your oxygen supply when you misuse his gifts? Aren't you glad that God doesn't give you only that which you remember to thank him for? (Has it been a while since you thanked God for your spleen? Me, too. But I still have one.) God's goodness is spurred by his nature, not by our worthiness. Someone asked an associate of mine, "What biblical precedent do we have to help the poor who have no desire to

become Christians?" My friend responded with one word: "God."[7]

Our precedent for serving our patients, even those who seemingly have no desire to adopt positive, healthy living or to become Christians, is God himself. As his vessels, we can be used mightily in his master plan if we follow his lead, obey him, and let him do his work in our patients' hearts as we treat them.

In your fight against cynicism, remember that God is your example, as well as the one whom you ultimately serve. In his strength, you can resist the pressure to turn your superiors into idols and care instead for your patients with the love of Christ.

Suggested Prayer

"Father, I confess that there are many times when I get caught up in the moment and begin complaining about the frustrations and annoyances that are before me. Sometimes I feel justified in doing so. Forgive me, Lord. Forgive my blinded, hardened heart. Melt it, and restore it once again to a heart that becomes a light for you. I falter so much, yet I know, Lord, that you pick me up again and walk with me every time I fall. For that, I give thanks and praise.

"Give me your Spirit to fight the negativity I encounter. Give me your strength to be a positive influence to fight the darkness. Remind me that you are sovereignly guiding my steps and that each person you put before me, no matter how rude, impatient, or uncaring, is a person marred and broken but still made in your image. Let me show these people your nature, your goodness, and your worthiness, and let your healing hands work through me. Even though I may not visibly see it, give me eyes of faith to see your kingdom being ushered here to these people."

Questions to Ponder

1. Why is the idea of helping people sometimes so much different from actually doing so?
2. Have you ever been in a situation in which you have been physically or emotionally exhausted, and even more seems to have been demanded of you? How did you respond?
3. What is your approach to interacting with people in the hospital who may respond to you in bitterness or cynicism?
4. How does knowing that God sovereignly guides your future give you strength to weather your trials in life?
5. Which truth about God can you meditate on that will keep you focused on loving and serving Christ today?

Chapter 18 Endnotes

1. F. W. Boreham, "Adoniram Judson's Life Text," *Wholesome Words*, http://www.wholesomewords.org/missions/bjudson11.html
2. *Helping the World to See*, 1.
3. "Battling the Unbelief of a Haughty Spirit," *Desiring God*, http://www.desiringgod.org/resource-library/sermons/battling-the-unbelief-of-a-haughty-spirit.
4. Fyodor Dostoyevsky, *The Brother's Karamazov* (New York: Penguin, 1993), 61–62.
5. Mother Teresa, *No Greater Love* (New York: New World Library, 1997) 29–30, 31.
6. *Helping the World to See*, 108.
7. *Helping the World to See*, 25–26.

CHAPTER 19

Choosing Your Career: The Value of Different Specialties

Few people know exactly what field of medicine they are going into before they begin medical school. The majority enter having only an inkling of what they might be interested in.

Keep an open mind, especially when first starting out. Various guides have been published to help you choose a specialty. There are books that tell you the nitty-gritty details of particular specialties and even discuss types of personalities that these specialties attract. There are exams that test your personality and help rank matching specialties to yours.

My medical school gave us one such survey, and on that day, neurosurgery was my number-one choice. Although I found it an interesting field, I also knew that there were many other factors that precluded me from going full-bore into that specialty, including the amount of time required for training and my interests outside of medicine. I constantly replayed my thoughts: *How do I know if what I'm interested in now will be what I'm interested in for the rest of my life? How do I know I'm not just "in the mood of the moment" and being influenced by what seems to be the limitless energy of my peers, making me want to choose a high-stress but impressive-to-others specialty? What if I end up so beaten-down and wiped-out by the stresses of medical school that I end up wanting to choose something low-stress that demands a lesser amount of energy—while, in the back of my mind, fearing that I may be missing out on God's best for me?*

Another reason people choose certain specialties is the money they can earn. To pay off school debt, they may end up choosing a higher-paying field, as opposed to the field they have a true passion for. Some choose their specialty for other reasons: the prestige, the honor of their peers, or to prove that they are better than others.

You can ask thousands of questions that trap you in the quicksand of second- and third-guessing. In fact, you can easily second- and third-guess yourself into ineffectiveness for God's kingdom. The problem is that these questions fail to consider the presence of a good and powerful Father who graciously and sovereignly guides and watches over you in spite of your sinfulness.

Do not dwell on the what–ifs or the lie that if you choose the wrong specialty, it will horribly affect the rest of your life. To do so is shortsighted and neglects the larger work of God. God will still use you, despite—and even through—your mistakes. You, of course, must do your part and seek his will in choosing a specialty, but realize that even your best intentions are often misguided or spotted with your own self-interest.

Tim Keller said it well: "We are more flawed and sinful than we ever dared believe, yet we are more loved and accepted than we ever dared hope at the same time."[1] You must submit your decisions wholly to God's cleansing grace, because "even your righteous deeds are like filthy rags" (Isa. 64:6). Remember, God can use mistakes—whether in motivation or deed—to ultimately bring him glory. If you find yourself wanting to switch specialties in the midst of residency or practice, it will take more work, but it is not impossible and can bring him honor. Sticking with your chosen specialty can also give him honor. The question is whether or not you will offer up every decision and motivation to him, seeking his will and glory in your life. This comes through a constant walking with God.

Know that God creates divine appointments with your patients and colleagues and that your calling is to be faithful where you are at this very moment. Will you obey, or will you be lost in the dark clouds of "where does God want me to go?," all the while ignoring his calling to serve those he divinely puts in front of you right now? We don't often make decisions with entirely pure motives, but to the extent of our ability, we must want to make his—not our own—glory known. He will honor that.

Picking Your Spiritual Specialty

When I was a university student, my pastor stated this simple truth: "Good theology leads to good doxology." In other words, an appropriate understanding and knowledge of who God is leads to appropriate and God-honoring worship of him. With this in mind, I want to encourage you not to think that only certain specialties honor God or can reflect the multifaceted nature of his character. What if you find yourself enjoying your anesthesia rotation but you think that only a general practitioner can talk to patients from a multifaceted patient perspective? After all, you can't explain the gospel to an anesthetized patient, right? Or how is it possible to express Christ's love as a radiologist? Aren't you just reading a film?

Questions like these may lurk in the back of our minds as we try to figure out which specialty we want to choose, but they also reveal how limited our vision is when it comes to extending and proclaiming the gospel to our patients. It is as if we believe that all a surgeon does is cut flesh with a scalpel. A surgeon is doing good in removing cancerous tissue from a body, being the hands of Christ to bring wholeness (the kingdom of God) through physical means. This also parallels the redemptive act of Christ in removing sin from within us and declaring us to be clean. The kingdom of God is brought into the world through both physical means (our body being healed from physical brokenness) and spiritual means (being forgiven and sanctified).

Likewise, an anesthesiologist reflects the character and compassion of Christ by bringing comfort and relief to anxious, hurting people. The preoperative discussion not only can put the patient at psychological ease but is also a unique opportunity to reflect the love of Christ to an anxious soul. Patients' feelings of empowerment often go out the window when they are gripped with the reality that they aren't in control of their own destinies—or heart rate, breathing, or ability to move, for that matter—while under anesthesia. In addition to providing physical comfort, meeting people in their time of humbleness allows the love of Christ to penetrate more deeply past the patients' illusion that they control their own futures. Praying with them, sharing the gospel message, speaking a comforting word, and providing a safe anesthetic are all ways an anesthesiologist can play his or her role in ushering the kingdom of God, bringing about physical and spiritual redemption with a whole-patient perspective.

You must work out your own practical doxology. There is so much more kingdom value to our work than the mentality that it's just a job to make money. How does the specialty that you are interested in, in its unique way, reflect the character, purposes, and heart of God? How can you see yourself as being Jesus to those you deal with in this specialty, with patients, nurses, colleagues, and others? You can be Christ through a specialty that has its own unique opportunities to meet the particular needs of a patient and those working around you.

All Specialties Are Interesting

During your rotations, you may find that all (or none!) of the specialties seem interesting to you. How can you decide? This can be both stressful and anxiety-provoking. *What do I choose if nothing really stands out to me? Will I really like any of these specialties in the long run? Can I see myself doing this five, ten, or fifteen years into the future?* Myriad questions can swirl in your mind.

Maybe you are the kind of person who wants to be absolutely sure before you take the big step of committing to a specialty. It is with this sense of uncertainty that you can follow the example of Abraham. "By faith Abraham, when called to go to a place he would later receive as his inheritance, obeyed and went, even though he did not know where he was going. By faith he made his home in the promised land like a stranger in a foreign country; he lived in tents, as did Isaac and Jacob, who were heirs with him of the same promise. For he was looking forward to the city with foundations, whose architect and builder is God" (Heb. 11:8–10).

Abraham had no idea where he was going, although he would eventually end up in the land of Canaan. The only thing he knew was the God he served, and by faith he was going to trust God in leading him wherever he would go. In the same way, you may not know which specialty you will end up in, but the more important question is whether you, like Abraham, will choose to walk faithfully with God.

God also made a promise to Abraham just before he left home: "I will make you into a great nation, and I will bless you; I will make your name great, and you will be a blessing. I will bless those who bless you, and whoever curses you I will curse; and all peoples on earth will be blessed through you" (Gen. 12:2–3). Do you trust that God will not only guide you but will also bless you if you choose to walk with him? You may not know where you will end up, but if you will only choose to trust him, your future will be more secure than if you try to procure it on your own.

Suggested Prayer

"Lord, picking my specialty seems like a huge deal to me. It's my profession. It's what I may be doing, if you will it, until I retire many years from now. Things seem so uncertain. There are times when I feel as if I don't know what I want to do or which specialty to go into. I pray for your wisdom and grace in making this choice. Give me peace and trust in this. Give me eyes to see how I can praise you in practical ways in whatever specialty I end up choosing. But I know that more than any specialty I go into, Lord, you want me to live in obedience. So I come before you and pray that I would be faithful even today. Guide my ways, Lord, and in my obedience, let me go forth in faith."

Questions to Ponder

1. Think about the specialty or group of specialties you think you are interested in. What is it about each one that you feel drawn to? What about each may concern you?
2. How can you approach choosing your specialty with a God-glorifying and God-trusting perspective?
3. How does the example of Abraham encourage a medical student who has no idea what specialty he or she wants to pursue?

4. Think about the phrase "good theology leads to good doxology." How can your specialty interest be a kingdom-glorifying, God-exalting way to honor and praise God?

Chapter 19 Endnotes

1. Tim Keller, "The Meaning of the Gospel," *The Gospel in Action*, http://extendingthekingdom.org/?page_id=17.

CHAPTER 20

Growing in Your Calling: The Subinternship

Doing my subinternship right now, and I have to admit, it's a bit scary that people actually take what I say seriously. I'm the person who writes the admissions notes for patients when they come in, and the attendings and the residents and all the consults, I've noticed, go to my notes first, before they do anything. They're busy, busy, and they aren't as detailed in their histories and physicals as I am, so they rely on my notes and my suggested recommendations as their starting points.

The first time I saw a consult reading my note, my gut went, "Ah, crud! What did I leave out? What did I miss? What did I completely miss? What did I forget to order?" I guess it's one of those learning experiences that all med students must and should go through, but when my name appears on the chart as the person taking care of patient John Doe, there's that added sense of fear and privilege, particularly when the nurse calls to tell me about a problem with that patient and the dreaded next words I hear on the phone are: "Well, what do you want to do for him?"

—Eric's journal entry: February 20, 2005

A subinternship is a rotation in which you act as a first-year resident, also known as an intern. Some people joke that this is a time during which you are a preattending or, tongue-in-cheek, "pretending." A subinternship involves having patients under your direct care. The nurses will usually go directly to you with any concerns regarding your patients, and with some oversight, you will make the decisions regarding which labs to order, what medicines to give, and what procedures to do. This is truly the time when you will be challenged to synthesize and apply what you have learned over the last several years.

Naturally, a lot of fourth-year students face this rotation with trepidation because of the amount of responsibility involved. This is understandable. After all, when you are under the protective umbrella of other residents, the opportunity to practice medicine can never be quite as in-your-face as when a nurse calls you in the middle of the night with, "Mr. Jones in room 204 has a low sodium level and is complaining of abdominal pain. What do you want me to do with it?" As much as we may want to say, "I think you have the wrong pager number" or "Take two aspirin and call me in the morning," you are being challenged to make decisions based on your growing knowledge base to care for your patients.

When you put on the white coat and take on the responsibilities of being a doctor, you will truly begin to experience what it means to practice medicine. Despite having a foundation of knowledge (to which you will add on a daily basis), you may feel initially that you are just acting the part. "This is the way I've seen it done, and it makes sense, so I'll order these meds and tests for my patient." Like breaking in new shoes, making your own decisions that directly impact your patient isn't easy at first. You are acting with the help of other medical students, residents, and attendings, based on what you know, but the learning process may chafe and rub you in very uncomfortable ways.

As you keep your mind open, however, you will find your role as an intern becoming more and more manageable, and then even comfortable. But this will not happen overnight. Medicine is changing, and staying abreast of current medical practice is a lifelong process. Just realize that it can be an enjoyable process, once the kinks and rough edges begin to wear down.

A subinternship lets you practice being someone you are already in the process of becoming. Read that last sentence again. As a fourth-year medical student with a basic understanding of medicine, you have the tools to be able to transfer what you know into the actual practice of diagnosing, treating, and caring for your patients. You will take that knowledge and grow in it as you mature in your profession and enter residency.

In a similar way, we as Christians are growing in understanding and maturity as we walk the Christian life. Peter tells us, "His divine power has given us everything we need for a godly life through our knowledge of him" (2 Peter 1:3). In other words, we can live and grow in godly maturity, because God has already given us the power to do so. You have been given the "white coat" of Christ's cleansing forgiveness, and now you have been called to "continue to work out your salvation with fear and trembling, for it is God who works in you to will and to act in order to fulfill his good purpose" (Phil. 2:12–13).

This "coat" of Christ is, however, not just what you do, but who you are. This is very important to understand. You may not feel like being a Christian sometimes, especially when a resident or attending yells at you or when you are post-call after running around the hospital all night. But being a child of God is not based on feeling. It is simply who you are. If you feel like dirt on the bottom of your resident's boot, remind yourself, "I am deeply loved and valued by the Great

Physician, and I have everything I need as his servant and his child. It is by his strength that I will continue and carry on serving him." If you experience times of desperation or feelings of inadequacy, know that nothing can separate you from the love of God and that you can continue living for his glory and in his strength.

As you exercise your role as a doctor during your subinternship, remember the parallel truths of becoming more like Christ. Just as there are challenging opportunities in taking on responsibilities and growing as a physician, there are also challenging opportunities in serving God and growing in maturity in him. When you put on the coat of an intern, you begin to act like one. When you put on the coat of Christ, you begin to act like him. Day-by-day, as you exercise the power he has given you to live for him and seek to know him, you can develop the character and the heart of the one whose coat you wear—Christ himself.

Suggested Prayer

"Lord, it can be challenging taking care of patients with the amount of responsibility I have as a subintern. I feel as if I'm still in the process of learning, and not having all the answers can be nerve-racking. Give me your wisdom as I take care of these patients. Help me to fill my white coat in my role as a doctor. Let me take care of my patients with confidence and humility. Thank you that you are making me more and more like Christ. Thank you that you have given me your Spirit so that I can, in your strength, live out my life for you. Grant me discipline to know my patients well, to study up and learn from them, and to grow in the knowledge of medicine."

Questions to Ponder

1. Think about someone you looked up to while you were in medical school. What did you like about that person that made you want to emulate him or her?

2. As you prepare to do your subinternship, what about the rotation do you think makes you the most excited? What is the most challenging or difficult? What steps can you take to meet these challenges?

3. "A subinternship lets you practice being someone you are already in the process of becoming." What does the spiritual analogy of your becoming more like Christ teach you when you feel inadequate or struggle with trying to live the Christian life?

4. When you are stretched to take on more responsibility during your subinternship, how can your understanding of what you are becoming in Christ help empower you to serve your patients, residents, and attendings?

CHAPTER 21

Match Day:
The Divine Appointment

Success is sweet, but grace is even sweeter.
—Pastor Eric Molicki

It was the one phone call that I'd prayed I would never get. "Eric, I've got some bad news." It was March of my senior year, and the dean's office was calling. "I'm really sorry to tell you this, but you did not match. Come to the office, and we'll see what we can do."

When I'd applied for a competitive residency, I had entertained the thought of not matching, but I had never seriously considered that it would happen. The devastation I felt when I got the call on Black Monday, the Monday before match day, was overwhelming. How could God allow something like this? I had worked so long and hard in medical school. Why wasn't he giving me this thing I wanted so desperately? Couldn't he oblige me with this one sweet morsel for all the good I thought I had been doing for him? I felt instead as if I had swallowed a very large and very bitter pill. God hadn't kept his part of our unspoken bargain!

For those not familiar with the process, most medical students undergo "the match" when applying to residency programs. This involves students ranking a list of residency programs for which they have interviewed, and in turn, the programs rank the students they have interviewed. Once students submit the rank list, they can only sit back, often nervously, and wait for the results. A computer program then uses an algorithm to make the best possible match between the two.

Depending on the specialty and the strength and compatibility of the student, he or she may get a "match" anywhere between their first and last choice. Some may not match at all. Waiting to find out the results can be a time of consternation, no matter how certain one might be about his or her chances of getting into a residency program.

Looking back, I believe there were two important truths I learned from my experience. First, just as Jesus said in Luke 18:19, "No one is good—except God alone." I had to realize that any godly thought I had and any good deed I had done came solely as a result of his working through me. I could not take credit for his sustaining me through the long days and nights of medical school, and as a result, I could not demand payback from him. Yet I acted as if God owed me something. "I served you faithfully! Now I think I deserve this one thing I really want." This is a subtle yet devastating lie that can lead one down the road of bitterness when things don't turn out the way one wants.

The other lesson was that God's plan will not always be the same as my own. I may see something as good, but God sees something else as even better. This certainly was the case for me in my initial choice of specialty, ophthalmology. Performing operations such as cataract surgeries was the perfect representation of the light of Christ giving sight to the spiritually blind. I enjoyed doing procedures, and I knew that on medical missions a significant number of sight-saving surgeries could be done in just a short period of time. Why *wouldn't* God want me to do something like that? And yet he closed that door. It felt as if he was denying me my birthright—the very thing

I had come to medical school to do. (This wasn't really true, but at the time, it felt like it.)

In his sovereign wisdom, he carried me through those uncertain times of scrambling for a position, and it was by his grace that he opened another door. I came to match day, thinking that I was in for a long day, perhaps needing to take a year off—and I had good reason to think that, believe me! But despite my fears of not having anywhere to go, it was in God's wise providence that he provided an opening in an entirely new specialty. I was certainly a recipient of his grace, because I didn't deserve the blessing he provided: both in an internship and a residency program. Despite my being a sinner who struggled with sin daily in thought and deed—manifested in my sense of self-righteous entitlement, anger, and bitterness for not matching—he suddenly made his direction clear to me.

I began that week feeling lost, confused, and ashamed, only to realize later that I was a recipient of such sovereign grace that it was truly hard to comprehend. I remember thinking, *Things may change, and they probably will, but in my feeble state, he has graciously given me a direction to go.* It was as if the road far ahead had been kept dark, but the path before me had been revealed, like a lantern showing me only where to take the next step.

It was during those humbling times that I began to learn that all God expected of me was to follow him and trust him daily and to do my best work unto him, whatever that work happened to be. God opened my eyes to this new specialty, and I knew that giving it my best in residency would honor God. That was why I came to the conviction that *it really matters less what specialty you practice than practicing whatever specialty you end up in with your utmost for his glory.*

As you wait to hear the good (or maybe not-so-good) news on match day, instead of passing the time wringing your hands or gnashing your teeth, realize that this is where the rubber of your faith meets the road. This is an opportunity to exercise your faith and give glory to the one who not only knows your outcome but who planned it. Instead of stress and worry, use the time for personal reflection and prayer. Ask yourself: *Where am I really placing my hope? Is all my joy and happiness grounded in where I end up next year? Is my personal worth and value dependent on if and where I match? If I don't match, how will I feel?*

If the match process doesn't turn out as you expect or hope, it is normal to feel sad or disappointed, but to feel totally crushed and ashamed, as I did, can be an indication that you are placing your worth in your professional status and other people's opinions of you, rather than in being a son or daughter of God. My thinking went this way: *I didn't match, and therefore I don't deserve respect from anyone— not my peers, not myself, and not even God. I don't want anyone to know, because their view of me will change, and they will look down on me. I am worthless and dumb compared to my classmates who matched. That is what shames and embarrasses me.*

Visceral feelings like these may seem to smolder constantly, but you must fight them, because they are the lies of the culture and the Devil. You must remember that your worth is based entirely on what Christ has already done for you at the cross. His love for you is unconditional, no matter what you have or have not accomplished. Trusting in his sovereign goodness means exactly that. He *knew* this was coming. In fact, he *planned* it. So trust him. Believe in the sovereignty of God. You are his dear child, and he has a unique plan, made especially for you alone, whatever your match outcome may be.

I will say it again: trust in his sovereign goodness. He may have you walk through a time of suffering and darkness, but this is so that you will see his power at work in your weakness. Let him be glorified in your weakness, and you will find a contentment and peace in him that will transcend any satisfaction you might get from matching even your first choice.

If you do match in one of your top choices, then by all means praise him! All good things come from him, and he has planned this that you might give him the glory. Whatever the outcome, he alone is able to provide the deep fulfillment and significance you crave. Don't let the world convince you that your name or your status before others is paramount. Seek to honor God and trust him with the consequences. "Show me your ways, O Lord, teach me your paths; guide me in your truth and teach me, for you are God my Savior, and my hope is in you all day long" (Ps. 25:4–5).

Suggested Prayer

"Father, this is the time when things are out of my hands. I've given my best effort on my applications and during my interviews, and now I entrust this match day to your hands. You are God. I am not. As much as I want a particular residency program and specialty, it's really your glory and purpose for my life that matters most. Whatever the outcome, I know and trust that it is in your hands and according to your sovereign purpose. Whether it means going to my first choice, needing to do a little more work, or even completely reevaluating my options, I want you to be glorified in me during this time. Your ways are sometimes mysterious, but you are not. You are always good! Let my obedience and heart serve you and you alone. You are my ultimate fulfillment, and may your good work always and continually be done in and through me, whatever the outcome."

Questions to Ponder

1. What are of some of your fears as you think about match day? Whether or not our fears are grounded in truth, why does the prospect of potential failure tend to consume us?
2. What changes in your thinking, if any, are needed to have a godward, God-glorifying perspective as you approach match day?
3. After you submit your rank list, think of specific ways you can honor and further God's kingdom as you wait for the results.
4. Consider praying for your and your classmates' futures, that God would glorify himself in each of your lives and give you faith in his good and sovereign plan. How can you serve others and be an encouragement to those who may be struggling in the match process?

CHAPTER 22

The Last Days ...

Finally! Your fourth and final year of medical school is coming to a close. It's been a long road of seemingly endless hours of library study and early morning travel for hospital rounds. You have had your fill of doing interviews. You have probably made your decision about where to go for residency, and the question that may be swirling in your mind is, "What should I do in these last couple months of medical school?" There may be electives or some required rotations that need to be finished, but it's around this time that you begin to let out a slow sigh of relief. Match day is over, and you know you are going to be somewhere, at least for the next year.

Here is a three-pronged approach you might take to the end of your fourth year: looking back at the past, looking at where you are now, and looking forward to the future.

Looking Back

You probably have developed some meaningful friendships in medical school. Don't let worries about the future keep you from nurturing and deepening those friendships. God has brought those friends into your life for a purpose. It can be easy to ignore them when you are wondering, "Where will I find housing? Will I be able to make it as an intern? How will I move all the stuff I've accumulated?"

As exciting as this time is, enjoy your time with the ministries, the fellowship, and the church of which you have become a part. Invest your time and energies in the relationships you have built. Before you leave school, make a commitment to be a blessing to those around you. Pray that God will give you a motivation and heart to say, "I have been a witness of Christ to my classmates and friends through my heart, words, and actions."

Right Now

You haven't graduated yet. As you wrap up rotations, beware of medical school senioritis. It can be a pain if the elective you thought you could skip out on was the reason the school administration gave you such a hard time graduating. Seek to learn, even in the specialty rotations you think you may never work in again. A good doctor isn't one who knows a lot about his own specialty and nothing about all the others. A good doctor is one who sees the interconnectedness of varying specialties, especially as they relate to his or her own. It is a good witness and a blessing to your attendings when you seek to learn from them, particularly when they know that you will not be pursuing their specialty. It sets you apart from your peers who choose not to show up or who give a halfhearted effort, which essentially is like saying, "This specialty to which you have devoted your professional life is of no interest or value to me." How sad it would be to miss this opportunity to learn from the experts in the field! It really is a win–win situation when you maintain your efforts. You are a good witness to your attendings, and you learn from them as well.

Looking to the Future

Residency is a whole new beginning for you, with new colleagues, new responsibilities, and a new "MD" or "DO" added to your name! A lot of practical issues need to be addressed before you start: How will you get to the hospital? Will you have a car, travel by public transport, or live close enough to walk? Will you buy a house or rent? Ship your belongings or sell them? Pack them in the car or U-Haul, or hire movers? You can ask your fellow graduates for help during the moving process, especially if they will be in the same city or hospital as you. See if you can find out who else will be joining your program and whether you can meet up before residency starts to establish rapport and begin new friendships. You can also get an idea from them (or from the residency program itself) where most of the residents choose to live and travel from.

If you are concerned about whether you will be able to remember anything from medical school, there is one thing you can be certain of: you will see common things over and over again, and your clinical acumen with each patient will improve as you grow in your skills.

Also, it is helpful to review your advanced cardiovascular life support (ACLS) skills! A medical school alumnus (who went on to become a medical supervisor for the television show *Scrubs*) once recounted an incident that occurred while he was an intern and a code blue was called. Typically, the first doctor who arrives at the scene has to assess the situation and run the code, and there are very few interns who want to do this. As he was running to the code, he suddenly took a profound interest in the headlines of a newspaper he was passing. Another intern caught him red-handed, but only after he admitted that he himself had tied and retied his shoelaces four times before responding to the call!

It can be too easy to get caught up in the worries of what will happen several months from now. Instead, look to the one who holds your future in his hands. God knows exactly what your residency experience will be like. He knows exactly who will be your first and last patient (and everyone in between), their diagnoses, and how to treat them.

Meditate on this: the God who promised to sustain you through medical school will also sustain you through residency and when you become an attending. God will not be surprised by your mistakes or any urgently ill patients who come your way. When your confidence is placed in the Great Attending, he will guide you through residency, and your hope can be grounded in his unshakable wisdom, goodness, and love.

Suggested Prayer

"As I finish up my rotations, Lord, I want to thank you, first of all, for getting me this far. You have promised to be faithful to me always, and I thank you for that comforting truth. Help me not to forget the relationships I have forged here in school and to continue to invest and be strengthened in the friendships made here and in church. Help me to be consistent in my rotations as I finish up. It can be tempting not to go, but help me to honor these attendings with whom I will finish up my rotations, and give me an open mind to learn from them. And, Father, I lift up to you my future in residency. You know every patient you will put before me. In these next growing, fruitful, and challenging years, I trust my training, my patients, and my life to your loving hands. To you, Lord, be all the glory, honor, and praise!"

Questions to Ponder

1. If you are in your last days of medical school, take a moment to look back and see how far you've come. You may have had some regrets and some deep joys as well. Commit this to God in prayer, realizing that he can redeem your experiences as a medical student—the good, the bad, and the ugly.

2. Even as you count down the last few months of school, what steps can you take to still be a good witness to your attendings? As tempting as medical school senioritis is, why is it not a good mentality to give in to?

3. With all the practical aspects of residency that need to be figured out, how does grounding yourself in the sovereignty of God help you face the future with true confidence and bright hope?

About the Authors

Eric Huang graduated from Brown University's selective eight-year medical program, receiving his bachelor's degree in cellular neuroscience and medical degree from Brown's Alpert Medical School in Providence, Rhode Island. He attended University of Connecticut for his residency in anesthesiology and currently practices in very sunny ("but it's a dry heat"), central California. He lives happily with his wife and young son, Elliott. They hope to have nine more children so they can have a total of two volleyball teams, as both Eric and his wife enjoy playing and would find it much easier than just joining a summer league. They are involved with their church and love the families God has brought into their lives there. If you would like to discuss the book with him, he can be reached at BeyondStudying@gmail.com.

Richard Chung graduated from Harvard University with a bachelor's degree in cognitive neuroscience. He received his medical degree from the Yale School of Medicine in New Haven, Connecticut and completed his residency in Internal Medicine-Pediatrics at Duke University and his fellowship in Adolescent and Young Adult Medicine at Children's Hospital Boston. He currently lives in North Carolina with his wonderful wife and two children. They, however, are not considering having a volleyball team at the moment.

Follow us on facebook at

www.facebook.com/BeyondStudying

CPSIA information can be obtained at www.ICGtesting.com
Printed in the USA
BVOW03s2230100414

350297BV00001B/5/P